...ould be returned on or before the date shown below. Items
...requested by other borrowers may be renewed in...
...phone. To renew, please quote...
...online a PIN is required...

REAL FOOD
KIDS WILL LOVE

Annabel Karmel

REAL FOOD KIDS WILL LOVE

Over 100
simple and
delicious recipes
for toddlers
and up

bluebird
books for life

First published 2018 by Bluebird
an imprint of Pan Macmillan
20 New Wharf Road, London N1 9RR
Associated companies throughout the world www.panmacmillan.com

978-1-5098-8842-9
A CIP catalogue record for this book is available
from the British Library
Printed and bound in Italy

Publisher Carole Tonkinson
Project Editor Laura Nickoll
Design Nic & Lou
Senior Editors Katy Denny and Martha Burley
Assistant Editor Hockley Raven Spare
Senior Production Controller Ena Matagic
Prop Styling Emma Lahaye
Food Styling Natalie Thomson

CONTENTS

INTRODUCTION

My approach to family cooking has always been that you don't need to cook 'food for kids', you simply need to cook real food that the whole family will love – nourishing meals that are wholesome, unadulterated and devoid of flavour enhancers, preservatives or additives.

It is easy to underestimate how adventurous little people can be when it comes to new tastes but children learn new skills on a daily basis so why not new foods? Too often – due to lack of time or fears over children going hungry – parents end up cooking a limited number of tried-and-tested meals. While I'm all for clean plates, this can often lead to fussy eating habits in children. This book provides you with a raft of new recipes to add to your repertoire that are simple to prepare but will broaden their food horizons.

FITTING IT ALL IN
We all know how important it is to keep the family fuelled on the right foods, but making time to pack in that all-important goodness is often easier said than done, especially with today's jam-packed schedules, when parents are wearing more hats and spinning more plates than ever before. As my three children were growing up, I often found myself scrabbling for time to prepare wholesome meals around starting up my business, devising new recipes and managing the kids' social calendars (which were often busier than mine!). After-school activities, play dates, work commitments, emails and other activities all take a bite out of the amount of time we spend eating together as a family. Cooking for your family is about making memories as well as menus – in years to come the smell of a fish pie could transport your children back to

> Cooking for your family is about making memories as well as menus.

the kitchen table of their youth; the taste of pasta bake or finger lickin' chicken wings might remind them of post-match muddy knees and toad in the hole may be remembered as a welcome sight after a puddle-splashing Sunday stroll. Though many of us aspire to this level of evocative eating, the reality is that parenting is often more chaos than fine cuisine.

The frantic nature of modern life can detract from the dinner table and our efforts to get everyone eating together. We all know that sitting down as a family is about more

> Sitting down as a family is about more than food – it is about connection and conversation, eye contact and intimacy; it is about being in the moment with the ones you love.

than food – it is about connection and conversation, eye contact and intimacy; it is about being in the moment with the ones you love. Finding enough time in the day to cook up this aspirational atmosphere can be challenging, but the good news is it takes less effort than you might think. My mission with this book is to empower and inspire you to give your family the best start in life with good honest food that diners young and old will love.

FOOD FOR EVERYONE

Catering to the different requests and requirements of your family may seem like the key to an easy life but it can leave you feeling like a short-order cook with no time to sit down and enjoy either your food or your family. If one of the reasons you don't eat as a family as often as you'd like is down to junior meals being too bland and boring for adult taste buds, I have good news! Each and every recipe in this book has been especially

designed to appeal to palates of all ages, so you can ditch the conveyor belt catering, rustle up real food that kids and the whole family will love, and perhaps introduce some new favourites for the big people, too.

Millions of families rely on my cookbooks at that all-important weaning stage, but there is no need for my books to be put back on the shelf once your babies are old enough to go to school: mums often tell me that they serve up my famous finger foods for dinner parties and my easy-to-follow style is perfect for students wanting to study over more than burnt toast and beans!

HEALTHY EATING

Healthy habits formed early in life set children on the best possible path and eating a wide variety of foods together at regular times is a good discipline to practise. Many of the meals, like my **Meatballs with Orzo** (page 145), are freezer friendly so you can make more

> Helping to prepare a family meal can do wonders for children's self-esteem and if they are involved in the cooking they are more likely to try the end result.

than you need and have them on standby for another day.

Half of all the food bought by families in the UK is now 'ultraprocessed' – made in a factory with ingredients you can't pronounce and additives invented by food technologists to generate products that bear little resemblance to the fruits, vegetables, meat, chicken and fish you would cook at home. Refined products such as pots of noodles with specks of dried meat and shrivelled vegetables loaded with salt and MSG, or snacks fortified with manufactured vitamins and minerals, washed down with sugary drinks, have lost virtually all their natural nutrients. We bear a responsibility to our children to allow them to grow up enjoying real food that sets them on a path of healthy eating that will last a lifetime.

KIDS IN THE KITCHEN
Helping to prepare a family meal can do wonders for children's self-esteem and if they

are involved in the cooking they are more likely to try the end result. OK, so inviting your pint-sized sous chefs to help in the kitchen could be a little chaotic, but the skills they'll learn will be well worth the slightly raised stress levels! Minimise the mess with a wipe-clean tablecloth, aprons and robust equipment like wooden spoons and plastic bowls. Give them simple tasks: children under three can mash with a fork or potato masher, stir ingredients, roll out dough and use plastic cutters to make shapes. Three- to five-year-olds can cut soft ingredients like bananas with plastic knives, tear herbs, hull strawberries and measure ingredients into a jug. They will enjoy cracking eggs and whisking and – of course – decorating cakes.

Once they are old enough to have mastered some basics, let your mini masterchefs loose in the kitchen to cook a meal by themselves. From the age of four, six and seven my three took it in turns to cook for everyone one day

> Cooking is great for naturally inquisitive young minds, feeds a thirst for foodie knowledge and teaches them about more than just a balanced diet.

a week – it gave them confidence and ensured they could make toast and scramble an egg as well as play a complicated computer game!

Cooking is great for naturally inquisitive young minds, feeds a thirst for foodie knowledge and teaches them about more than just a balanced diet: as they weigh and measure ingredients they are developing maths skills without even realising, and following recipe instructions and being mindful of utensils are both good life skills. Supervising children while they learn to use knives and avoid steam from a hot kettle is safer than not teaching them and leaving them to experiment without you.

Learning to cook from scratch is a great way to instil a real interest and understanding of what goes into the food you eat. Obesity is on the rise and allowing your children to cook a variety of meals will teach them about getting the balance right between indulgent treats and healthy options – and recipes like my **Teriyaki Beef Stir-Fry** (page 106) are so yummy they

won't feel short-changed by wholesome, healthy cooking.

The fun goes beyond the taste buds and the meal prep; encourage them to use chopsticks, show them where the dish they're eating originates on a map and how to load all those empty plates into the dishwasher (never the most popular part of mealtimes but polished-off plates should make your cooks proud!).

PORTION SIZES

While it's important for children to step up to the plate and help in the kitchen, it's worth noting that a large mound of food can be overwhelming for a little person, so try presenting plates of mini portions – dishes like my **Mini Toad in the Hole** (page 46) made in individual muffin tins, and my **Mini Chicken Burgers with Apple and Sage** (page 128) look fantastic. Individual portions are also a convenient way of freezing things so instead of making one large **Paella** (page 41) try freezing mini child portions in ramekins.

Did you know that children consume a third of their daily food intake at school? That's why I've also included a fantastic selection of lunchbox ideas.

MY RECIPES

Whether you meal-plan or meal-panic, whether you label yourself as a meat eater, vegan, vegetarian or flexitarian, whatever way you feed your family, there are times when the most important factor is speed; hungry mouths won't wait and with my 15-minute meals they won't have to! Stock your store cupboards and have a fridge of essentials and you can rustle up a **Butternut Squash Carbonara** (page 99) or **Butter Chicken** (page 24) in not much more time than it will take your tribe to lay the table.

Quick meals don't have to mean a nutritional compromise. Make your own healthy alternatives to 'Fast Food' with my **Mini Cauliflower Pizzas** (page 142) or my alternative to chicken nuggets, **Quinoa Baked Chicken Fingers** (page 130), which are easy to prepare and packed with goodness for your growing family. Likewise, with vegan and vegetarian food, gone are the days when these diet and lifestyle choices left you lacking; my **Sweetcorn and Cherry Tomato Pancakes** (page 72) or **Lentil Bolognese** (page 82) are fabulously filling and delicious. Don't be deterred by the myth that lentils require overnight soaking and a lot of faff, there are many pre-cooked and quick-cook options that make pretty instantaneous suppers – and they are good for your purse, too.

Did you know that children consume a third of their daily food intake at school? That's why I've also included a fantastic selection of lunchbox ideas – it is too easy for them to be packed full of the wrong things (the usual culprits: fat, sugar and salt) and not only miss the nutritional mark, but also negatively impact a child's energy and concentration levels for the rest of the day. Lunchbox inspiration can die a dreary death at 7am in the morning as you cajole your sleepy kids downstairs for breakfast. Instead, plan ahead: my **Frittata Muffins** (page 158)

> The fun, finger-food style recipes also double up as the perfect treats for play dates, too; children often want to re-fuel and run.

or **Turkey and Cucumber Roll-ups** (page 154) are infinitely preferable to a soggy white bread sandwich, and preparing food the night before will alleviate some of the morning madness while you try to get everyone out of the door on time. Something from last night's dinner can also re-appear as a coveted lunchbox treat the next day.

Too often a bruised apple or brown banana are returned to sender un-eaten; try making my **No-sugar Chocolate Orange Energy Balls** (page 188) – they are delicious and no one would know they are made with dates and cashew nuts. I've never seen those left on a plate! Or, incite lunchbox envy and get your child involved in making **Spiced Apple, Squash and Carrot Muffins** (page 190) to share with their buddies – hidden veggies never tasted so good! Soups and salads are perfect for lunchboxes, too. Flasks keep soup warm, and my **Tomato Soup with Pesto Swirl** (page 68) is a real winner on cold days. For lunchbox salads, keep dressing in a separate pot to

ensure they stay crisp. Ice packs or freezer gels, or frozen cartons or plastic bottles of juice, will keep things cool in the summer and provide a refreshing drink to cool kids down, too. Insulated lunchboxes keep the cold in and the heat out, which is good for regulating the temperature and keeping germs at bay, and a pack of wet wipes are always useful for sticky fingers.

The fun, finger-food style recipes also double up as the perfect treats for play dates, too; children often want to re-fuel and run so let them lunge at my **After-School Veggie Platter** (page 162) or grab a handful of **Chicken, Sweetcorn and Carrot Balls** (page 166). A hungry child is a less fussy child so that famished post-school window of opportunity is a good time to try something new. It is all too easy to get stuck in a rut and only offer a few favourite things but using this time when children are hungry to break the pattern and offer them something different is really important.

I'm a firm believer in enjoying a little of what you fancy. However, many of the seemingly indulgent treats in this book contain more healthy ingredients than you might think for something that looks and tastes so divine! Even my **Dairy-free Beetroot and Chocolate Cake** (page 191) packs in a punchy portion of your five-a-day and I challenge you to find a tastier 'free-from' chocolate cake. If your children haven't helped prepare it you can have fun asking them to guess the mystery ingredient ... even the most ardent 'beetroot hater' will be converted when you reveal it!

The pressure to find seasonal activities around the holidays can take the fun out of things for parents trying to entertain excited children; cooking up a festive treat together is a great way to keep them occupied and gives you some helping hands to get dinner ready too! The **Rudolph Potatoes** (page 220) are an easy way to transform an old favourite into something festive and inject some sparkle into your spuds.

The themed recipes in this book work really well for parties, too. Children love hands-on activities, and baking, building and decorating party food is a sure-fire way to keep them entertained. If you and your children get a taste for gatherings with goodies to eat you could encourage them to make invitations and decorations for events throughout the year; my **Doughball Christmas Wreath** (page 222) makes a show-stopping centrepiece and is perfect for little ones to assemble then eat; the **Dressed-up Cupcakes** (page 208) look (and taste) fantastic and Easter is perfect for cotton-tailed bunny invites and cute **Easter Cupcakes** (page 206).

Of course, you don't need to wait for the holidays as an excuse to make cooking together the activity of choice; combine children and the ideas in this book and you have an activity, education and delicious meal any day of the year! I've spent over twenty-five years supporting millions of families by creating quick, easy and tasty recipes and I've learnt that with a little inspiration and support, everyone can cook a good meal. I really do believe that mealtimes should be simple and shareable, and I hope this book leaves you believing and achieving that too.

COOK'S NOTES

For fan-assisted ovens reduce the oven
temperature by 20°C.

———

All eggs are medium unless otherwise stated.

———

All recipes for 4–6 people feed a family of
2 adults and 2+ children, and all 2-portion
recipes are adult-sized.

———

Take care to always wash your hands, knife
and chopping board in hot soapy water after
preparing poultry.

———

For best results when baking cakes use butter
and eggs that are at room temperature.

———

Season recipes lightly – avoid adding
too much salt.

CHAPTER 1

FAMILY FAVOURITES

POT-ROAST CHICKEN

If I'm cooking for a crowd there is nothing better (or more satisfying) than a one-pot recipe – just chuck in all the ingredients and leave it to do its thing while you get on with other jobs or spend time with the kids. This pot-roast chicken is a delicious, easy, all-in-one meal that feeds the whole family. If you don't want to use wine (although the alcohol evaporates in the cooking process) you could simply use 600ml/1 pint of stock.

2 tbsp sunflower oil
2 leeks, sliced
2 large carrots, diced
2 garlic cloves, crushed
200ml/7fl oz white wine
400ml/14fl oz chicken stock
2 tsp fresh thyme leaves
1 medium or large chicken
1 tbsp olive oil
350g/12oz new potatoes
10 fresh sage leaves
salt and pepper

Preheat the oven to 200°C/400°F/Gas 6.

Heat the sunflower oil in a shallow casserole dish over a medium heat. Add the leeks, carrots and garlic and fry for 3–4 minutes until softened, then add the wine and 200ml/7fl oz of the stock. Bring to the boil, add the thyme leaves, then add the chicken. Drizzle the chicken with the olive oil and season lightly with salt and pepper.

Roast in the oven for 30 minutes, then add the new potatoes and the remaining stock and roast for a further 30–45 minutes, or until the chicken is golden and cooked through.

Scatter with the sage leaves and serve.

BUTTER CHICKEN
WITH YELLOW RICE

We have a popular range of children's meals sold in supermarkets in Australia. My Butter Chicken is one of the bestselling dishes and is based on this very recipe. It's a mildly spiced tomato-based curry which is suitable for the whole family. Serve it with my yellow rice for the finishing touch on what is sure to become a favourite meal.

knob of butter
1 large onion, chopped
2cm/¾in piece of fresh root
  ginger, peeled and grated
2 garlic cloves, crushed
1 tsp garam masala
1 tsp ground cumin
1 tsp ground coriander
1 tsp sweet smoked paprika
2 tbsp tomato puree
200ml/7fl oz chicken stock
1 tbsp mango chutney
2 skinless chicken breasts, diced
1 tbsp sunflower oil
6 tbsp full-fat Greek yoghurt
salt and pepper
spring onion slivers,
  to garnish (optional)

YELLOW RICE
¼ tsp turmeric
200g/7oz basmati rice

To cook the yellow rice, put the turmeric in a saucepan of boiling water. Add the rice and stir, then reduce the heat and simmer for 12–15 minutes until the rice is just tender. Drain well and leave to steam in the sieve, covered, for 5 minutes.

To make the curry, melt the butter in a saucepan over a medium heat. Add the onion and fry for 3–4 minutes until softened, then add the ginger, garlic and spices. Cook for 30 seconds, then add the tomato puree and stock. Bring to the boil then reduce the heat and simmer for 10 minutes. Add the mango chutney and remove from the heat.

Season the diced chicken with a little salt and pepper. Heat the oil a frying pan until hot, then add the chicken and fry briefly until browned but not cooked through. Add the chicken to the sauce and simmer for 5–7 minutes until cooked. Stir in the yoghurt just before serving. Serve the butter chicken with the yellow rice and garnish with spring onion slivers, if you like.

The butter chicken can be frozen for up to 3 months. Cook from frozen for about 20 minutes at 180°C/350°F/Gas 4, or until warmed through, or defrost and heat through in a pan.

248 calories

CHICKEN BAKE WITH SLICED ROASTED POTATO TOPPING

This is a wonderfully comforting dish of tender chicken in a tasty sauce of sautéed leek and carrots topped with sliced roasted potatoes sprinkled with cheese and gratinated in the oven. It can be prepared ahead and reheated without losing any of its appeal.

25g/1oz butter
75g/3oz onion, chopped
75g/3oz leek, diced
100g/3½oz carrots, peeled and diced
25g/1oz plain flour
200ml/7fl oz chicken stock
150ml/5fl oz whole milk
25g/1oz parmesan cheese, grated
1 tbsp chopped fresh thyme
150g/5oz cooked chicken, diced
300g/11oz small potatoes, peeled and thinly sliced
1 tbsp sunflower oil
30g/1¼oz cheddar cheese, grated

Preheat the oven to 200°C/400°F/Gas 6 and line a baking tray with baking parchment.

Melt the butter in a saucepan over a medium heat, add the onion, leek and carrots and fry for 5 minutes until softened, then add the flour and stir over the heat for 1 minute. Gradually stir in the stock and milk and cook for a couple of minutes until smooth and thickened. Remove from the heat and add the parmesan cheese, thyme and diced chicken. Spoon into a baking dish.

Toss the potatoes with the oil and spread them out on the lined baking tray. Roast in the oven for 15 minutes until lightly golden. Remove from the oven and turn on the oven's grill setting to high.

Arrange the roasted potato slices on top of the chicken bake then sprinkle with the grated cheddar and cook under the preheated grill for a few minutes until the cheese is golden and bubbling, then serve.

CAULIFLOWER, HAM AND MACARONI CHEESE BAKE

Most kids I know love pasta and this dish, with its cheesy topping, promises to be another beloved recipe in your repertoire. Using half cauliflower and half macaroni is a quick and easy way to up your family's five-a-day. Cauliflower can be one of those tricky vegetables with fussy eaters but I assure you, it'll be smiles all round with this simple, bubbling-hot meal.

225g/8oz macaroni pasta
300g/11oz cauliflower florets
45g/1½oz butter
45g/1½oz plain flour
750ml/1¼ pints whole milk
1 tsp Dijon mustard
120g/4½oz mixture of grated
  gruyere, cheddar and
  parmesan cheeses
100g/3½oz diced ham

Preheat the oven to 180°C/350°F/Gas 4.

Cook the macaroni in a pan of boiling salted water according to the packet instructions, drain and rinse under cold running water.

Steam the cauliflower florets in a steamer for 7 minutes until just cooked, then leave to cool.

Melt the butter in a saucepan over a medium heat, add the flour and stir over the heat for 1 minute. Gradually pour in the milk, whisking constantly until the sauce is smooth and thickened. Add the mustard and two thirds of the grated cheese.

Mix the cooked macaroni, cauliflower, ham and cheese sauce together then spoon the mixture into an ovenproof dish and sprinkle with the remaining grated cheese.

Bake in the oven for 20 minutes until heated through and golden brown on top, then remove from the oven and serve.

The dish can be frozen after baking (once cooled) for up to 3 months. Cook from frozen for about 20 minutes at 180°C/350°F/Gas 4, or until warmed through.

TERIYAKI TUNA AND RICE

When something I make is gobbled up by my three children in less than 5 minutes I know it's good ... We all love Japanese food and the soy, sesame, ginger and honey tuna marinade in this recipe is utterly delicious.

4 x 250g/9oz tuna steaks, sliced
  into 10–12 thick strips

MARINADE
3 tbsp soy sauce
2 tsp good-quality balsamic
  vinegar
1½ tbsp honey
½–1 tsp sesame oil
1 tsp freshly grated root ginger

RICE
1 tbsp sunflower oil, plus extra for
  cooking the tuna
2 carrots, diced
1 onion, chopped
½ red pepper, deseeded and diced
150g/5oz white mushrooms,
  sliced
1 garlic clove, crushed
150g/5oz cooked and shelled
  edamame
1 tbsp sweet chilli sauce, plus extra
  to serve
250g/9oz cooked long grain rice
salt and pepper

Mix all of the marinade ingredients together in a bowl. Add the tuna and stir to coat the tuna in the marinade. Cover and leave to marinate in the fridge for 30 minutes.

Heat the oil for the rice in a frying pan over a medium heat. Add the carrot, onion, red pepper, mushrooms and garlic and fry for 3–4 minutes until softened, then add the edamame and sweet chilli sauce. Toss over a high heat for a minute, then season to taste with a little salt and pepper and remove from the heat.

To cook the tuna, heat a little sunflower oil in a separate frying pan. Remove the tuna from the marinade, add it to the pan and fry it for 1½–2 minutes until golden (it should still be a little pink in the middle).

Put the tuna on top of the rice in serving bowls or plates, then pour the marinade into the frying pan you cooked the tuna in and gently heat until bubbling. Pour the sauce over the tuna and rice and serve with extra sweet chilli sauce.

VARIATION
Sesame Teriyaki Tuna with Rice
Cut the tuna into 1.5cm/¾in cubes instead of strips, marinate it as above, then fry for about 30 seconds to seal before rolling the cubes in 3 tablespoons of sesame seeds and serving with the rice and sauce.

SALMON IN A PARCEL

This quick, healthy and delicious recipe uses just a handful of ingredients. Give the salmon a lift with a squeeze of lemon and some fresh pesto before wrapping it up all nice and snug, ready to be baked.

4–6 new potatoes
100g/3½oz French beans, halved
8 cherry tomatoes, halved
6 fresh basil leaves
2 skinless salmon fillets (about
   100g/3½oz each)
2 generous tbsp fresh green pesto
squeeze of lemon juice
salt and pepper

Preheat the oven to 180°C/350°F/Gas 4.

Cook the new potatoes in a pan of boiling salted water for 12–15 minutes until tender, then remove with a slotted spoon. Cut the potatoes into quarters once they are cool enough to handle.

Blanch the French beans in the same pan of boiling water for 3–4 minutes, drain and refresh in cold water.

Cut 2 large squares of foil and place them on a large baking sheet.

Divide the potatoes, green beans, tomatoes and basil between each square of foil, putting them in the centre of the foil, and season lightly with salt and pepper. Place a salmon fillet on top of each and squeeze some lemon juice over them. Spread a tablespoon of pesto on top of each. Fold in the edges of the foil to meet in the middle and seal.

Bake in the oven for 15 minutes. Remove from the oven, open the parcels and remove the salmon skin before serving.

FISH PIE TWO WAYS

I absolutely love fish pie and so do my readers: they have even been serving up my fish pies from my baby and toddler cookbooks for their dinner parties. Here's a delicious version for the whole family to enjoy.

40g/1½oz butter
75g/3oz leek, thinly sliced
1 large onion, finely chopped
2 tsp white wine vinegar
3 tbsp plain flour
200ml/7fl oz fish stock
150ml/5fl oz whole milk
juice of ½ lemon
30g/1¼oz parmesan cheese,
  grated
1½ tsp chopped fresh dill
200g/7oz skinless salmon fillet,
  diced
200g/7oz skinless cod fillet,
  diced
salt and pepper

TOPPING OPTIONS
150g/5oz block ready-made
  shortcrust pastry
1 egg, beaten with a little milk
OR
150g/5oz carrots, sliced
650g/1lb 6oz floury potatoes,
  peeled and diced
knob of butter

Preheat the oven to 200°C/400°F/Gas 6.

Melt the butter in a saucepan over a medium heat, add the leek and onion and cook, stirring, for 10 minutes until softened. Add the vinegar and stir over the heat until it has evaporated, then add the flour and stir for a minute. Gradually pour in the milk, stirring constantly, until the sauce is smooth and thickened. Remove from the heat, add the lemon juice, parmesan and dill and season lightly with salt and pepper. Add the fish and stir. Spoon into a small ovenproof dish and top with your chosen topping.

For the Pastry Topping
For the pastry topping, grate the block of pastry over the fish mixture, brush the pastry with egg wash and bake in the oven for 20 minutes until bubbling and lightly golden on top.

For the Carrot and Potato Topping
For the carrot and potato topping, cook the carrots in a pan of lightly salted boiling water for 20 minutes while you're making the white sauce and cook the potatoes in a separate pan of lightly salted water for 15 minutes, until cooked. Drain the carrots and potatoes, mash them together with the butter and season to taste. Spread the topping over the fish and bake in the oven for 20 minutes until bubbling and lightly golden on top.

The fish pie can be frozen (once cooled) for up to 2 months. Defrost, then reheat in a preheated oven at 180°C/350°F/Gas 4 for about 20 minutes, or until heated through.

GLAZED SALMON WITH CHINESE-STYLE VEGGIE RICE

We design a range of family meals for a well-known home delivery food company where you get all your ingredients in a box and a menu card with easy step-by-step instructions and this meal is a great favourite. The salmon marinade makes it very moreish and, of course, salmon is packed with those all-important omega 3s.

2 skinless salmon fillets, cut into cubes
1 tbsp sunflower oil
small knob of butter
1 large banana shallot, finely chopped
1 carrot, finely diced
½ red pepper, deseeded and finely diced
1 garlic clove, crushed
250g/9oz cooked long grain rice
40g/1½oz cooked garden peas
3 tbsp tinned sweetcorn
1 tbsp soy sauce
1 tbsp sweet chilli sauce
salt and pepper

SAUCE
1 tbsp tomato ketchup
1 tbsp soy sauce
1 tbsp sweet chilli sauce
1 tsp white wine vinegar

Preheat the oven to 180°C/350°F/Gas 4.

Mix all of the sauce ingredients together in a small bowl. Put the salmon cubes on a piece of foil in a small roasting tin. Pour over the sauce and seal the foil to make a parcel. Bake in the oven for 15 minutes.

While the salmon is cooking, heat the oil in a wok or large frying pan over a medium heat. Add the butter, then add the shallot, carrot and red pepper and fry for 3 minutes until softened. Add the garlic and fry for 30 seconds, then add the rice, peas and sweetcorn and fry for 2 minutes until the rice is hot. Add the soy sauce and sweet chilli sauce and season with a little salt and pepper.

Spoon the rice onto plates, arrange the baked salmon on top and drizzle over the sauce in the foil.

COCKTAIL SAUSAGE CASSEROLE

Every family has a go-to casserole dish for those nights when all you crave is comfort food, and here's mine, made with cocktail sausages!

2 tbsp olive oil

1 onion, chopped

1 red pepper, deseeded and diced

1 carrot, finely diced

2 garlic cloves, crushed

400g/14oz tin chopped
   tomatoes

1 tbsp sun-dried tomato paste

1 tsp chopped fresh sage leaves

1 tsp chopped fresh thyme leaves

dash of Worcestershire sauce

pinch of sugar

12 cocktail sausages

Preheat the oven to 180°C/350°F/Gas 4.

Heat the oil in a saucepan over a medium heat, add the onion, pepper and carrot and cook, stirring, for 5 minutes until softened, then add the garlic and fry for 30 seconds. Add the tomatoes, tomato paste, herbs and Worcestershire sauce and sugar, cover and simmer for 10 minutes.

Put the sausages on a baking sheet and cook in the oven for 15 minutes until lightly browned.

Add the browned sausages to the sauce, cover and simmer for a further 10 minutes.

Serve the casserole with potatoes or rice.

The casserole can be frozen (once cooled) for up to 3 months. Cook from frozen for about 20 minutes in the oven at 180°C/350°F/Gas 4, or until warmed through.

MEATLOAF WITH QUICK TOMATO SAUCE

Introducing you to the mighty meatloaf. Ideal for feeding a crowd, it's the perfect 'smiles all round' supper for the whole family. The secret ingredient? I add grated apple to give the dish a natural sweetness kids will love.

MEATLOAF

200g/7oz white bread (fresh or stale)

6 tbsp milk

75g/3oz carrot, grated

1 apple, peeled and grated

1 onion, chopped

500g/1lb 2oz minced beef

4 tbsp tomato ketchup

1 tbsp soy sauce

1 tbsp Worcestershire sauce

2 tbsp chopped fresh thyme leaves

salt and pepper

QUICK TOMATO SAUCE

400g/14oz tin chopped tomatoes

2 tbsp tomato ketchup

2 tbsp sun-dried tomato paste

2 tsp Worcestershire sauce

1 garlic clove, crushed

1 tbsp chopped or torn fresh basil leaves

Preheat the oven to 180°C/350°F/Gas 4 and lightly grease a 900g/2lb non-stick loaf tin.

Blitz the bread in a food processor until it forms fine crumbs. Tip the crumbs into a bowl, add the milk and set aside for 5 minutes, then tip the soaked breadcrumbs back into the processor with all the remaining ingredients. Season with a little salt and pepper and blitz briefly until well combined. Spoon the mixture into the tin, level the top and bake for 1¼ hours, covering the meatloaf with foil after 45 minutes if necessary, to prevent it burning.

Meanwhile, put all the sauce ingredients in a saucepan, bring to the boil, then reduce the heat and simmer for 5 minutes.

Turn the meatloaf out of its tin onto a baking sheet. Put the meatloaf back into the oven for 10 minutes to brown the top.

Cut into 8 slices and serve with the tomato sauce.

The meatloaf can be frozen (once cooled) for up to 2 months. Wrap it in heavy-duty foil then pop it into a plastic box with a lid or a freezer bag. Freeze the sauce separately in a plastic box.

BEEF CASSEROLE
WITH FIVE VEGETABLES

You can't go wrong with this cosy and comforting winter warmer. It's also a great dish to up your family's all-important iron intake.

3 tbsp sunflower oil
800g/1¾lb lean diced
    stewing beef
1 onion, finely chopped
1 leek, finely chopped
2 carrots, thinly sliced
1 garlic clove, crushed
2 tbsp sun-dried tomato paste
4 tbsp plain flour
450ml/15fl oz beef stock
leaves from 2 rosemary sprigs,
    finely chopped
1 tsp dried oregano
150g/5oz butternut squash,
    peeled and diced
150g/5oz parsnips, peeled
    and diced

CARROT AND POTATO MASH
800g/1¾lb potatoes, peeled
    and diced
350g/12oz carrots, peeled
    and diced
generous knob of butter
1–2 tbsp milk
salt and pepper

Preheat the oven to 140°C/275°F/Gas 1.

Heat 1 tablespoon of the oil in a casserole dish over a high heat. Brown the beef in batches, then set aside.

Heat another tablespoon of the oil in the casserole dish, add the onion, leek and carrots and fry for 2–3 minutes until softened. Add the garlic and fry for 30 seconds, then add the tomato paste and flour and stir for a minute. Return the beef and any juices in the bowl to the casserole and stir to coat. Add the stock and herbs, stir, cover and bring to the boil, then place in the oven for 1½ hours, or until the beef is tender. Remove from the oven and increase the temperature to 200°C/400°F/Gas 6.

Put the squash and parsnip on a baking sheet, toss with the remaining oil and roast for 20 minutes until golden, then add to the casserole. While they are cooking, boil the potatoes and carrots in separate pans (cook the potatoes for 15 minutes and the carrots for about 10 minutes) until both are tender. Drain, return to the pans and mash. Mix the potato and carrot with the butter and milk, mash and season lightly with salt and pepper.

Serve the beef casserole with the carrot and potato mash.

The casserole can be frozen (once cooled) for up to 3 months. Cook from frozen for about 20 minutes in the oven at 180°C/350°F/Gas 4, or until warmed through.

BEEF MASSAMAN CURRY WITH ROASTED SWEET POTATO

If you're craving a curry night then look no further. This dish is bursting with aromatic flavours and has a silky, lightly spiced sauce that the whole family will love.

2 tbsp sunflower oil
350g/12oz sirloin steak, sliced
 into strips
1 onion, finely chopped
1 tsp grated fresh root ginger
1 tbsp red Thai curry paste
400g/14oz tin coconut milk
1 tsp fish sauce
pinch of brown sugar
squeeze of lime juice
3 dried lime leaves
salt and pepper
cooked rice, to serve

ROASTED SWEET POTATO
400g/14oz sweet potatoes,
 peeled and diced
1 tbsp olive oil

Preheat the oven to 200°C/400°F/Gas 6.

Toss the diced sweet potato and olive oil on a baking sheet and season lightly with salt and pepper. Roast in the oven for 25 minutes.

Heat 1 tablespoon of the sunflower oil in a large frying pan over a high heat. Season the steak strips lightly with salt and pepper and fry for 1–2 minutes until browned and sealed. Transfer to a plate and set aside.

Heat the remaining sunflower oil in the pan over a medium heat. Add the onion and cook for about 3 minutes until softened, then add the ginger and cook for 1 minute. Add the remaining ingredients, bring to the boil and simmer for 5 minutes.

Add the roasted sweet potatoes and browned beef to the pan and cook gently for 2–3 minutes. Remove the lime leaves and serve with rice.

The curry can be frozen (once cooled) for up to 3 months. Cook from frozen for about 20 minutes at 180°C/350°F/Gas 4, or until warmed through, or defrost and heat through in a pan.

MACARONI BOLOGNESE BAKE

Family favourite alert! A classic bolognese always goes down a treat, particularly when paired with macaroni – another hands-down favourite.

225g/8oz macaroni
25g/1oz cheddar cheese, grated

BOLOGNESE SAUCE
1 tbsp sunflower oil
1 onion, chopped
1 carrot, finely diced
2 garlic cloves, crushed
500g/1lb 2oz lean minced beef
2 tbsp tomato puree
2 x 400g/14oz tins cherry
  tomatoes
1 tsp dried oregano
1 tbsp chopped fresh basil leaves
salt and pepper

CHEESE SAUCE
40g/1½oz butter
40g/1½oz plain flour
450ml/15fl oz whole milk
50g/2oz parmesan cheese, grated
½ tsp Dijon mustard

Start by making the bolognese sauce. Heat the oil in a large saucepan over a medium heat, add the onion and carrot and fry, stirring, for 5 minutes until softened, then add the garlic and minced beef and fry until browned, breaking up any lumps with a wooden spoon. Add the tomato puree and stir for 30 seconds, then add the cherry tomatoes and oregano. Bring to the boil, reduce the heat, cover and simmer for 45 minutes until the mince is tender. Add the basil and season lightly with salt and pepper.

Cook the macaroni in a pan of boiling salted water according to the packet instructions, drain and rinse under cold running water.

Preheat the oven to 180°C/350°F/Gas 4.

To make the sauce, melt the butter in a saucepan over a medium heat, add the flour and stir for a few seconds. Gradually add the milk, whisking constantly for about 2 minutes until the sauce is smooth and thickened, then stir in the parmesan and mustard.

Mix the bolognese sauce and pasta together, spoon into a large ovenproof dish or individual dishes, spread the cheese sauce on top and sprinkle with the grated cheddar. Bake in the oven for 25–30 minutes until golden and bubbling.

The bake can be frozen (once cooled) for up to 3 months. Defrost, then reheat in the oven at 180°C/350°F/Gas 4 for 15–20 minutes, or until heated through.

ENCHILADAS

Here's a Tex Mex favourite your whole family will love. Serve it as it is or with some crème fraîche or sour cream and salsa alongside.

---

6 medium tortilla wraps or
8 mini tortilla wraps
1 x quantity Bolognese Sauce
(see page 39)
75g/3oz cheddar cheese, grated
olive oil, for greasing and brushing
crème fraîche, sour cream and
salsa (see page 67), to serve
(optional)

Preheat the oven to 200°C/400°F/Gas 6 and grease a large ovenproof dish with oil.

Put the wraps on a board. Spoon one eighth or one sixth (depending on how many wraps you're using) of the bolognese sauce along one side of a wrap and sprinkle with a little cheese. Roll up the wrap and place in the greased dish. Continue with the remaining bolognese and wraps, leaving behind a little cheese for sprinkling on top.

Brush the wraps with a little oil, sprinkle with the remaining cheese and bake in the oven for 20 minutes until golden and crisp.

Serve with crème fraîche, sour cream and salsa, if you like.

PAELLA

Bursting with bright colours, this dish is sure to catch the eye of any hungry tums in your midst. It's also packed with lots of chicken, seafood and veggies for a nutritious boost.

2½ tbsp sunflower oil

2 onions, chopped

½ red pepper, deseeded and diced

2 garlic cloves, crushed

½ tsp sweet smoked paprika

¼ tsp turmeric

1 tsp tomato puree

100g/3½oz white mushrooms, sliced

250g/9oz paella rice

900ml/1½ pints chicken stock

1 skinless chicken breast, diced

80g/3oz cooked squid rings

100g/3½oz cooked small prawns

50g/2oz frozen peas

3 tbsp tinned sweetcorn

1 tbsp chopped fresh thyme leaves

juice of ½ small lemon

salt and pepper

Heat 1½ tablespoons of the oil in a large frying pan over a medium heat, add the onions, red pepper and garlic and fry for 3–4 minutes, then add the paprika, turmeric, tomato puree and mushrooms and fry for 2 minutes. Add the rice and stir to coat it in the mixture, then add the stock, bring to the boil, reduce the heat and simmer gently for 15 minutes until the rice is almost tender.

Meanwhile, heat the remaining oil in a small frying pan and fry the chicken for 2 minutes on each side, or until cooked.

Add the chicken to the paella with the squid, prawns, peas, sweetcorn, thyme and lemon juice, cook for a further 5 minutes until heated through, then remove from the heat. Season to taste with a little salt and pepper and serve.

The paella can be frozen (once cooled) for up to 3 months. Cook from frozen for about 20 minutes at 180°C/350°F/Gas 4, or until thoroughly warmed through, or defrost and warm through in a pan.

TASTY BEEF WITH
5 VEGGIES AND RICE

Refuel after a long day with my simple one-pot wonder – jam-packed full of colourful veggies, this quick and easy recipe transforms minced beef into a seriously scrumptious family meal.

1 tbsp olive oil
100g/3½oz courgettes, diced
100g/3½oz red pepper, deseeded and diced
100g/3½oz red onion, diced
100g/3½oz chestnut mushrooms, diced
1 garlic clove, crushed
250g/9oz lean minced beef
1 tsp dried oregano
1 tbsp sun-dried tomato paste
400g/14oz tin chopped tomatoes
20g/¾oz parmesan cheese, grated
200g/7oz cooked long grain rice
1 tbsp fresh chopped basil leaves

Heat the oil in a saucepan over a medium heat, add the vegetables and fry for 5 minutes until softened, then add the garlic and cook for 30 seconds. Add the minced beef and fry it with the vegetables until browned, breaking up any lumps with a wooden spoon. Add the oregano, tomato paste and chopped tomatoes and bring to the boil. Reduce the heat, cover and simmer for 30 minutes until the mince is tender.

Stir in the cheese, then stir in the rice until heated through. Remove from the heat, add the basil and serve.

The dish can be frozen (once cooled) for up to 3 months. Defrost, then reheat in the oven for about 20 minutes at 180°C/350°F/Gas 4, or until hot, or heat through in a pan.

ROAST LEG OF LAMB WITH NEW POTATOES

Bring the family together to tuck into this mouthwatering Mediterranean-style roast leg of lamb.

1 leg of lamb (about 2kg/4½lb)
1 garlic clove, sliced
3 rosemary sprigs
6 sun-dried tomatoes in oil, plus
   4 tbsp oil from the jar
1 small butternut squash, peeled,
   deseeded and cut into
   2.5cm/1in chunks
2 red peppers, deseeded and cut
   into chunks
sea salt and pepper

ROAST NEW POTATOES
500g/1lb 2oz new potatoes,
   scrubbed and halved if big
2 tbsp olive oil
2 garlic cloves, bashed (skin
   left on)
2 rosemary sprigs

Preheat the oven to 190°C/375°F/Gas 5.

Cut slits all over the lamb with a sharp knife and insert slices of garlic and a few rosemary leaves. Season the lamb with a little salt and pepper, place it in a large roasting tin and arrange the remaining rosemary sprigs around the leg. Drizzle the lamb with 2 tablespoons of sun-dried tomato oil.

Roast the lamb for 45 minutes, then add the squash, peppers and sun-dried tomatoes and another 2 tablespoons of sun-dried tomato oil to the tin and stir to coat them in the lamb juices. Turn the lamb over, then place back into the oven for another 45 minutes until the squash and pepper are soft and lightly golden and the lamb is cooked through.

For the potatoes, put all the ingredients into a shallow roasting tin with a little salt. Toss to coat in the oil, then roast at the same time as the leg of lamb for 40–45 minutes until crisp. Season with pepper.

Remove the lamb and potatoes from the oven and leave the lamb to rest for 10 minutes covered with foil. Serve the potatoes with the lamb.

MINI TOAD IN THE HOLE

Transform a traditional hearty British dish into one ideal for little fingers – kids will love to have their very own mini version of this much-loved meal. They also make great canapes.

---

12 cocktail sausages
100g/3½oz plain flour
2 eggs
175ml/6fl oz whole milk
sunflower oil, for greasing

Preheat the oven to 200°C/400°F/Gas 6 and brush a 12-hole muffin tin with oil.

Put the sausages on a baking sheet and roast them in the oven for 10–15 minutes until nearly cooked and very lightly golden.

Whisk the flour, eggs and milk together in a large bowl with an electric hand-held whisk until smooth. Transfer the batter to a jug.

Put the greased tin in the oven for 10 minutes to get very hot, then remove it and immediately pour the batter mixture into the holes, until they are each half-filled with batter.

Put a cocktail sausage in the middle of each hole filled with batter, put back in the oven and cook for 15 minutes until well risen and golden brown.

ROAST BEEF WITH MINI YORKSIRE PUDDINGS AND ONION GRAVY

My perfect Sunday is going for a walk in the countryside with my three dogs (a golden retriever, Samoyed and Spaniel), then coming home to cook up lunch for friends and family. Roast beef with all the trimmings? Who could resist...

1.4kg/3lb beef topside
a few rosemary sprigs
800g/1¾lb floury potatoes, peeled and cut into chunks
3 tbsp sunflower oil
500g/1lb 2oz baby carrots
1 tsp maple syrup
salt and pepper

ONION GRAVY
2 tbsp sunflower oil
1 onion, finely chopped
3 tbsp plain flour
400ml/14fl oz beef stock
½ tsp Worcestershire sauce
1 tsp tomato puree

Preheat the oven to 200°C/400°F/Gas 6.

Season the beef and place it in a roasting tin. Put some rosemary sprigs around the joint and roast for 20 minutes per 500g/1lb 2oz plus an additional 20 minutes. Remove the beef from the oven and leave to rest.

While the beef is in the oven, parboil the potatoes in a pan of boiling salted water for 4 minutes, then drain. Put 2 tablespoons of the sunflower oil in a baking tray and place in the oven for 2 minutes to get hot. Remove the tray from the oven, add the potatoes and toss them in the oil. Return the tray to the oven and roast for 35 minutes until golden and crisp, turning them over after 20 minutes.

Put the carrots in another roasting tin. Toss them with the remaining tablespoon of sunflower oil and season with a little salt and pepper. Roast for 30 minutes until lightly golden, then drizzle with the maple syrup and put back into the oven for a further 5 minutes. Reserve the juices from the roasting joint of beef.

To make the gravy, heat the sunflower oil in a saucepan over a medium heat. Add the onion and saute for 4–5 minutes, then add the flour and whisk over the heat for a few seconds.

Gradually add the stock, whisking continuously until smooth. Add the juices from the beef roasting tin, Worcestershire sauce and tomato puree, bring to the boil and whisk for about 2 minutes until smooth and thickened. Carve the beef into thin slices and serve with the vegetables, gravy and mini Yorkshire puddings, and green vegetable of your choice.

MINI YORKSHIRE PUDDINGS

Makes 30–36 mini
Yorkshire puddings

sunflower oil
85g/3¼oz plain flour
2 eggs
125ml/3¼oz whole milk

Preheat the oven to 200°C/400°F/Gas 6.

Drizzle a little oil into 30–36 holes of two 24-hole mini muffin tins and put the tins in the oven for 5 minutes to get hot.

Whisk the flour, eggs and milk together in a large bowl with an electric hand-held whisk until smooth. Transfer the batter to a jug.

Remove the tins from the oven and immediately pour the batter mixture into the holes, until they are each half-filled with batter. Bake in the oven for 12–15 minutes until well risen and crisp.

ROAST CHICKEN WITH BUTTERNUT SQUASH, THYME AND SAGE STUFFING BALLS

Making time to eat together at the dinner table as a family is so important and a Sunday roast is the ultimate excuse. You'll be surprised just what younger members will be willing to try when everyone sits down and eats together. The butternut squash stuffing is super tasty, too.

1 large corn-fed, free-range or
  organic chicken
salt and pepper

MARINADE
2 tbsp olive oil
2 tbsp soy sauce
juice of ½ lemon
leaves from 1 rosemary sprig,
  chopped
1 garlic clove, sliced

ROAST POTATOES
750g/1lb 12oz floury potatoes,
  peeled and cut into large chunks
3 tbsp sunflower oil
1½ tbsp finely chopped rosemary
  leaves

Mix the marinade ingredients together in a large bowl (big enough to fit the chicken). Add the chicken and coat it in the mixture, then leave to marinate at room temperature for at least 20 minutes.

Preheat the oven to 180°C/350°F/Gas 4. Place the marinated chicken in a roasting tin. Roast in the oven for 1½ hours, covering it with foil after 45 minutes, until golden and cooked through and the juices run clear when you pierce the thickest part of a thigh with a sharp knife.

To make the roast potatoes, put the potatoes in a saucepan, cover with cold water, add a pinch of salt, bring to the boil and cook for 5–6 minutes until firm but just starting to soften. Drain thoroughly, tip back into the pan and shake to roughen the surface of the potatoes. Drizzle the sunflower oil into a large roasting tin and heat it in the oven. Once it's hot, remove the tin from the oven, add the potatoes and coat them thoroughly in the oil. Sprinkle with the chopped rosemary and roast for 30–40 minutes, turning them once, until golden and crispy. Drain on kitchen paper and season lightly with salt and pepper.

BUTTERNUT SQUASH STUFFING

1 tbsp olive oil

1 leek, roughly chopped

75g/3oz butternut squash, peeled and grated

1 carrot, grated

1 tbsp chopped fresh thyme leaves

1 tbsp chopped fresh sage leaves

150g/5oz fresh white breadcrumbs

1 egg yolk (optional)

GRAVY

2 shallots, finely chopped

1 tbsp red wine vinegar

3 tbsp plain flour

450ml/15fl oz chicken stock

1 tsp Worcestershire sauce

1½ tsp soy sauce

pinch of brown sugar

While the chicken and potatoes are in the oven, make the stuffing balls. Heat the olive oil in a frying pan over a medium heat, add the leek and fry for 5 minutes, until just softened. Remove from the heat and transfer the cooked leek to a bowl. Add the remaining stuffing ingredients (leave out the egg yolk if you like) and season lightly with salt and pepper. Shape the stuffing mixture into 12 balls, place on a baking sheet lined with baking parchment and bake in the oven for 20 minutes.

Remove the chicken from the oven and transfer it to a serving plate to rest, covered with foil.

To make the gravy, strain the chicken roasting juices and fat from the roasting tin – there should be about 3 tablespoons. Heat the chicken fat (keep the juices) in a saucepan over a medium heat, add the shallots and fry them for 5 minutes until softened, then add the vinegar and reduce for 10–15 seconds. Stir in the flour and cook for a minute, then gradually stir in the stock and the chicken juices. Whisk for a couple of minutes until the gravy is thickened and smooth. Add the Worcestershire sauce, soy sauce and sugar and simmer for 2 minutes.

Serve the chicken and stuffing balls with the roast potatoes and gravy and a green vegetable of your choice.

TIP

To make breadcrumbs out of stale bread, blitz the bread in a food processor then freeze the crumbs in a plastic bag. You can then scoop out as many grams as you need straight from the freezer.

BEEF CROQUETTES

I'm all about using up those leftovers! So, if you have any roast beef (see pages 48–9) going spare, transform it into these tasty croquettes. They are super tasty and you can freeze them once cooked and cooled, simply reheating them in the oven when needed.

150g/5oz cooked mashed potatoes, cooled
75g/3oz cold roast beef (see pages 48–9), finely chopped
50g/2oz carrot, grated
2 spring onions, finely chopped
1 tsp chopped fresh thyme leaves
1 tsp sun-dried tomato paste
a few drops of Worcestershire sauce
50g/2oz fresh white breadcrumbs
2 tbsp sunflower oil
salt and pepper

Put all of the ingredients (except the oil) in a bowl, season lightly with salt and pepper, then mix until well combined. Shape into 6 sausage shapes.

Heat the oil in a frying pan over a medium heat, add the croquettes and fry for 3–4 minutes, turning them until lightly golden all over and heated through. Alternatively, bake them in an oven preheated to 180°C/350°F/Gas 4 on a greased baking sheet for 12 minutes.

The cooked croquettes can be frozen (once cooled) for up to 3 months. Defrost, then reheat for 10–12 minutes in the oven at 180°C/350°F/Gas 4, or until warmed through.

CHICKEN AND VEGETABLE CROQUETTES

This is a delicious way to use up leftover roast chicken (see pages 52–3). With a crunchy crumb coating and a tasty soft filling this finger food is super scrummy. You can substitute sweet chilli sauce for the ketchup and add a teaspoon of soy sauce for an oriental variation.

200g/7oz cooked mashed potatoes, cooled
100g/3½oz cooked chicken, finely diced
4 spring onions, thinly sliced
1 carrot, grated
1 tsp chopped fresh thyme leaves
50g/2oz cheddar cheese, grated
1 tbsp tomato ketchup
2 tbsp sunflower oil
salt and pepper

COATING
3 tbsp plain flour
1 egg, beaten
30g/1¼oz panko or dried breadcrumbs

Put the mashed potato, chicken, spring onions, carrot, thyme, grated cheese and ketchup in a bowl and season lightly with salt and pepper. Mix to combine and mould into 10 sausage shapes.

To make the coating, put the flour in one bowl, the beaten egg in another bowl and the breadcrumbs in a third bowl. Coat each croquette in flour, then the egg, then the panko breadcrumbs.

Heat the oil in a large frying pan over a high heat, add the croquettes and fry for about 4 minutes until golden on all sides and heated through.

The cooked croquettes can be frozen (once cooled) for up to 3 months. Cook from frozen for 15–20 minutes in the oven at 180°C/350°F/Gas 4, or until warmed through.

CHAPTER 2

MEAT-FREE
&
VEGAN

RIGATONI WITH TOMATO, BASIL AND MOZZARELLA

This veggie pasta is easy to prepare and passes the taste test with flying colours.

2 tbsp olive oil
1 onion, finely chopped
½ red pepper, deseeded and finely diced
2 garlic cloves, crushed
600g/1lb 5oz tinned chopped tomatoes
1 tbsp tomato puree
1 tsp honey
3 tbsp chopped fresh basil leaves
2 tbsp mascarpone
40g/1½oz Italian hard cheese, grated
150g/5oz rigatoni pasta
50g/2oz mozzarella pearls
salt

Heat the oil in a saucepan over a medium heat, add the onion and pepper and fry for 10 minutes until softened. Add the garlic and fry for 30 seconds, then add the chopped tomatoes, tomato puree and honey and bring to the boil. Reduce the heat and simmer for 10 minutes, then remove from the heat and blitz until smooth with an electric stick blender. Add the basil, mascarpone and half the grated cheese.

Cook the pasta in a pan of boiling salted water according to the packet instructions, drain and add it to the sauce. Mix well and add the mozzarella.

Spoon the pasta and sauce into a small baking dish (or individual baking dishes), sprinkle with the remaining grated cheese and place under a hot grill for 5 minutes until the cheese is bubbling.

You can freeze the sauce for up to 6 months.

VEGETABLE AND LENTIL CURRY

You can play around with the amount of curry powder in this recipe depending on how hot you like your curry. If you want to make a vegan version replace the yoghurt or cream with either soya yoghurt or a non-dairy cream, or just leave it out.

1 tbsp olive oil

1 large onion, finely chopped

½ red pepper, deseeded and diced

2 large carrots, diced

150g/5oz butternut squash, deseeded and diced

1 garlic clove, crushed

1 heaped tsp mild Korma curry powder

300ml/10fl oz vegetable stock

75g/3oz dried red lentils

150g/5oz cauliflower florets

1 tbsp mango chutney

2 tbsp yoghurt or double cream

salt and pepper

cooked rice, to serve

Heat the oil in a saucepan over a medium heat, add the onion, pepper, carrots and squash and fry for 2 minutes, then add the garlic and fry for 30 seconds. Stir in the curry powder and fry for a few seconds, then pour in the stock and tip in the lentils. Bring to the boil then reduce the heat and simmer for 10 minutes. Add the cauliflower florets and simmer for 5–6 minutes until just tender.

Stir in the mango chutney and yoghurt or cream, season lightly with salt and pepper and serve with rice.

PENNE PASTA PRIMAVERA

The basis of this recipe is the quickest and easiest foolproof light cheese sauce made with crème fraîche, vegetable stock and parmesan. Vary the vegetables depending on your preference. Almost anything goes: try butternut squash, asparagus, green beans, courgette ... the choice is yours.

180g/6oz small penne pasta
1 tbsp olive oil
1 red onion, sliced
1 red pepper, deseeded and diced
1 medium courgette, diced
1 garlic clove, crushed
150ml/5fl oz vegetable stock
100g/3½oz full-fat crème fraîche
100g/3½oz broccoli florets
60g/2¼oz parmesan cheese, grated
100g/3½oz cherry tomatoes, halved
2 tbsp chopped fresh basil leaves
salt and pepper

Cook the pasta in a pan of boiling salted water according to the packet instructions.

Meanwhile, heat the oil in a large frying pan over a medium heat, add the onion, pepper and courgette and fry for 5 minutes until slightly softened, then add the garlic and fry for 30 seconds. Add the stock and simmer until it has reduced by half. Stir in the crème fraîche and remove from the heat.

Add the broccoli florets to the pasta pan 4 minutes before the pasta is cooked, then drain the pasta and broccoli and add it to the frying pan.

Toss the pasta, broccoli and sauce together, then add the grated parmesan, tomatoes and basil. Season lightly with salt and pepper and serve straight away.

SWEET POTATO WEDGES WITH CORN SALSA

Sweet potatoes become so delicious when roasted in the oven and the edges caramelise from the release of their natural sugars. The sharp freshness of the corn salsa complements the sweetness of the potatoes perfectly. They are great as a nourishing snack or served as a tempting side dish, and are also suitable for vegans if you use a dairy-free Italian cheese – there are many good ones now available in supermarkets.

2 medium sweet potatoes, scrubbed and cut into wedges
2 tbsp olive oil
10g/¼oz Italian hard cheese (or vegan dairy-free hard cheese), finely grated
salt and pepper

SALSA
100g/3½oz drained tinned sweetcorn
½ red pepper, deseeded and diced
2 spring onions, sliced
10 cherry tomatoes, chopped
2 tbsp olive oil
1 tsp rice wine vinegar
½ tsp honey

Preheat the oven to 180°C/400°F/Gas 6 and line a baking sheet with baking parchment.

Put the potato wedges, oil and a little salt and pepper on the baking sheet and toss together to coat. Roast in the oven for 25 minutes, then turn the wedges over and sprinkle with the grated cheese. Roast for a further 5–10 minutes until golden and soft.

Put the salsa ingredients in a food processor and blitz for just 2–3 seconds until roughly chopped.

Serve the salsa with the baked sweet potato wedges.

TOMATO SOUP WITH PESTO SWIRL

Warm up tums with a soothing bowl of soup – the flavours of the tomato and pesto really are a match made in heaven. Serve with a wedge of crusty bread for some serious dipping.

1 tbsp olive oil
2 onions, chopped
2 garlic cloves, crushed
40g/1½oz sun-dried tomatoes in oil, chopped
2 x 400g/14oz tins chopped tomatoes
350ml/12fl oz vegetable stock
1 tbsp tomato ketchup
1 tsp sugar
100ml/3½fl oz double cream
4–6 tbsp fresh green pesto
salt and pepper
crusty bread, to serve

Heat the oil in a saucepan over a medium heat, add the onion and garlic and fry for 5 minutes until softened. Add the sun-dried tomatoes, chopped tomatoes, stock and ketchup. Season with a little salt and pepper and add the sugar. Cover, bring to the boil, reduce the heat and simmer for 15 minutes.

Blitz until smooth using an electric stick blender.

Spoon into bowls and drizzle each serving with a swirl of cream and pesto.

You can freeze the soup (once cooled) for up to 2 months. Defrost, then reheat in a saucepan until piping hot.

SWEETCORN
AND KALE FRITTERS

This is one of those foolproof recipes where everything just gets blitzed in the food processor then takes only a couple of minutes to cook. The delicious golden fritters are suitable for vegans.

198g/7oz tin sweetcorn, drained
30g/1¼oz trimmed kale
4 spring onions, chopped
1 garlic clove, crushed
1 tsp sweet chilli sauce
50g/2oz plain flour
½ tsp baking powder
2 tbsp sunflower oil

Put all the ingredients (except the oil) in a food processor and blitz until finely chopped.

Heat the oil in a frying pan over a medium-high heat. Spoon 4–5 separate tablespoons of the mixture into the frying pan and fry the fritters for 1–2 minutes each side until lightly golden and cooked through. Transfer to a plate lined with kitchen paper then continue frying the rest of the mixture to make a total of 10–12 fritters.

HIDDEN TREASURE QUINOA SALAD

In a quest to find the world's healthiest food it would be almost impossible to miss out one of the best complete protein sources: quinoa. Combine it with this delicious dressing for a king-of-the-superfoods salad that is perfect for vegans, vegetarians and anyone who wants a delicious power-packed lunch to set them up for the day.

120g/4½oz quinoa
4 tbsp tinned sweetcorn
½ red pepper, deseeded and
  diced
1 carrot, finely diced
½ red onion, finely diced
50g/2oz dried cranberries
50g/2oz pomegranate seeds
salt and pepper

DRESSING
2 tbsp orange juice
4 tbsp sunflower oil
2 tsp soy sauce
1 tbsp red wine vinegar
2 tsp maple syrup

Cook the quinoa in a pan of boiling water according to the packet instructions, drain and leave to cool.

When cold, spoon the quinoa into a serving bowl. Add the remaining salad ingredients and mix to combine.

Whisk the dressing ingredients together in a small jug. Pour the dressing over the salad, season lightly with salt and pepper and stir.

SPINACH AND CARROT BITES

These fantastic quick and easy vegan 'mini bites' encourage kids to eat their veggies and they are baked not fried, so they make for an even healthier take on a finger-food favourite.

sunflower oil, for greasing
150g/5oz baby spinach, washed
160g/5½oz carrots, grated
2 eggs, beaten
50g/2oz fresh breadcrumbs
50g/2oz dairy-free cheese, grated
3 spring onions, finely chopped
pinch of salt

Preheat the oven to 200°C/400°F/Gas 6 and line a baking sheet with baking parchment. Brush the parchment with oil.

Cook the spinach in a dry frying pan over a high heat for a minute or two until wilted. Remove from the heat, leave to cool, then squeeze out any liquid from the spinach, roughly chop and put in a bowl with the remaining ingredients. Mix to combine.

Spoon 12 mounds of mixture onto the lined baking sheet and bake in the oven for 12 minutes, or until firm and lightly golden.

You can freeze the cooked bites (once cooled) in a plastic container for up to 2 months. Defrost, then reheat in a preheated oven at 180°C/350°F/Gas 4 for about 20 minutes, or until heated through.

SWEETCORN AND CHERRY TOMATO PANCAKES

As a nod to my popular sweetcorn fritter recipes, I've included these savoury pancakes, which are just as delicious. Top with homemade salsa for some added oomph.

PANCAKES
175g/6oz self-raising flour
1 tsp baking powder
2 large eggs
150ml/5fl oz whole milk
75g/3oz Italian hard cheese or
    dairy-free cheese, grated
1 tbsp sun-dried tomato paste
6 cherry tomatoes, finely
    chopped
3 spring onions, finely chopped
100g/3½oz tinned sweetcorn
2 tbsp sunflower oil
salt and pepper

SALSA
12 cherry tomatoes, quartered or
    roughly chopped
2 spring onions, thinly sliced
2 tbsp finely chopped fresh
    basil leaves
2 tbsp olive oil
1 tsp white wine vinegar

Whisk the flour, baking powder, eggs and milk together in a large bowl until you have a smooth batter. Add all the remaining ingredients (except the oil), season lightly with salt and pepper and mix well.

Heat the sunflower oil in a frying pan over a medium heat, add heaped spoonfuls of the batter mixture, fry for 2 minutes, then flip over and cook on the other side for 2 minutes until lightly golden and cooked through.

Mix all of the salsa ingredients together in a bowl and season with salt and pepper.

Serve the pancakes with the tomato salsa.

SCRAMBLED EGGS WITH SPINACH AND GRUYERE

Scrambled egg really is the breakfast of kings! Hearty, filling and tasty, the gruyere cheese elevates this weekend favourite to delicious new heights.

knob of butter, plus extra
  for spreading
50g/2oz spinach
2 large eggs, beaten
4 tbsp milk
30g/1¼oz gruyere cheese,
  grated
1 English muffin, halved

Heat a small frying pan over a medium heat until hot. Add half the butter and the spinach and fry for a few minutes until the spinach has wilted. Transfer the spinach to a chopping board and roughly chop.

Mix the eggs and milk together in a bowl. Add the remaining butter to the pan, pour in the egg and stir for a minute or so until scrambled. Add the grated gruyere and spinach and remove from the heat.

Lightly toast the split muffin, spread with butter and spoon the eggs on top. Serve straight away.

VEGETABLE STIR-FRY WITH MARINATED TOFU

Introduce your children to new flavours with this tasty vegetable and tofu stir-fry. Tofu is a really versatile ingredient and also a great source of protein. Marinate the tofu in soy sauce and maple syrup and add to stir-fried veg for the ultimate super speedy midweek meal.

100g/3½oz medium egg noodles
200g/7oz broccoli florets
2 tbsp sunflower oil, plus extra for frying the tofu
2 red onions, thinly sliced
2 garlic cloves, crushed
pinch of dried chillies (optional)
1 yellow pepper, deseeded and thinly sliced
250g/9oz shiitake mushrooms, thinly sliced
1 tbsp soy sauce
1 tbsp fish sauce
2 tbsp sweet chilli sauce
2 tsp lime juice

MARINATED TOFU
2 tbsp soy sauce
1 tbsp maple syrup
180g/6oz firm tofu, cut into 1.5cm/¾in cubes
2 tbsp plain flour

Mix the soy sauce and maple syrup for the marinade together in a bowl. Add the tofu, coat it in the mixture and leave it to marinate at room temperature for 30 minutes.

Cook the noodles in a pan of boiling water for 5 minutes, adding the broccoli florets for the last 3 minutes of cooking time. Drain and rinse under cold running water for a few seconds.

Heat the 2 tablespoons of sunflower oil in a wok over a medium heat, add the onion, garlic and chilli (if using) and fry for 3 minutes, then add the yellow pepper and mushrooms and stir-fry for 2–3 minutes. Add the noodles and broccoli to the vegetables in the wok. Heat through then remove from the heat.

Mix the soy sauce, fish sauce, sweet chilli and lime juice together and pour it over the noodles and veg in the wok.

Pour sunflower oil into a frying pan to a depth of 1cm/½in and place it over a high heat. Put the flour in a bowl, drain the tofu then gently coat it in the plain flour. When the oil is hot, fry the tofu on all sides for 2 minutes until browned, then add it to the stir-fry and heat everything through again, briefly. Serve immediately.

QUESADILLA WITH TOMATO, BASIL AND MOZZARELLA

A classic Italian margherita pizza in the form of a quesadilla. The fresh flavours combined with warm melting cheese are a match made in heaven (they're also the perfect finger food for toddlers).

6 mini tortilla wraps
1½ tsp sun-dried tomato paste
60g/2¼oz mature cheddar cheese, grated
60g/2¼oz mozzarella, grated
2 small tomatoes, thinly sliced
3 tsp chopped fresh basil leaves
1 tsp sunflower oil

Put 3 wraps on a chopping board. Spread half a teaspoon of sun-dried tomato paste over each wrap and top with the cheeses, tomato slices and basil. Put the remaining 3 wraps on top to make 3 sandwiches.

Heat the oil in a frying pan over a medium heat, add a quesadilla and fry for 2–3 minutes until lightly golden on the outside and melted in the middle. Turn the quesadilla over and fry for a further 2–3 minutes. Repeat with the remaining 2 quesadillas and serve straight away.

MY FAVOURITE VEGAN BURGERS

Sneaking vegetables into a burger is a good option for children who are super fussy and profess to hate veggies. Watch them munch these vegan burgers up in blissful ignorance. Instead of using egg as binder in the burger mixture, I use chia seeds soaked in water.

2 medium carrots, grated

1 medium courgette, grated

50g/2oz chestnut mushrooms, finely chopped

½ tsp dried oregano

1 tbsp chopped fresh flat-leaf parsley leaves

pinch of cayenne pepper

1 tbsp tomato ketchup

½ tbsp soy sauce

150g/5oz fresh brown breadcrumbs

1 tbsp chia seeds or 1 tsp egg substitute powder

2 tbsp sunflower oil

salt and pepper

soup or salad, to serve

Put the grated carrot and courgette in a clean tea towel and squeeze out the excess liquid. Transfer to a bowl and add the mushrooms, oregano, parsley, cayenne pepper, ketchup, soy sauce and 100g/3½oz of the breadcrumbs. Mix well and season with a little salt and pepper.

Put the chia seeds (if using) in a small bowl with 3 tablespoons of cold water and leave for 5 minutes until thickened. Add the mixture to the vegetables in the bowl or, if using egg substitute, mix the powder with 2 tablespoons of cold water then add it to the mixture.

Shape the mixture into 8 burgers and coat each burger in the remaining breadcrumbs.

Heat the oil in a large frying pan over a medium heat and fry the burgers in batches for 2–3 minutes on each side until golden and crisp. Serve with soup or salad.

The cooked burgers can be frozen (once cooled) for up to 2 months. Defrost, then reheat in a preheated oven at 180°C/350°F/Gas 4 for about 20 minutes, or until heated through.

MINI TOFU AND VEGGIE BURGERS

These vegetarian burgers are delicious. You can make them vegan by opting for dairy-free cheese. Serve them with vegetables; perhaps broccoli, sugar snap peas, baby carrots or stir-fried veg. If you wish, make the mixture into 8 larger burgers.

350g/12oz sweet potato
75g/3oz brown mushrooms, finely chopped
85g/3oz carrots, grated
4 spring onions, sliced
100g/3½oz firm tofu, diced
50g/2oz crackers, crushed (I use Matzo or Jacobs)
2 tsp soy sauce
30g/1¼oz Italian hard cheese, grated
plain flour, for coating
sunflower oil, for frying

Prick the sweet potato with a fork and bake it in an oven preheated to 200°C/400°F/Gas 6 for 35–40 minutes until soft.

When the sweet potato is cool, cut it open and scoop the flesh out into a bowl. Add all the remaining ingredients except the flour and oil, stir to combine and shape into 15 mini burgers.

Coat the burgers in flour. Heat a little oil in a frying pan over a medium heat. Fry the burgers in batches for 2–3 minutes on each side until golden.

CAULIFLOWER, BROCCOLI AND SAGE BURGERS

Kids love to pick up food with their hands and these veggie burgers are also bursting with nutritious goodness. Everyone's a winner!

sunflower oil, for greasing
150g/5oz cauliflower florets
100g/3½oz broccoli florets
50g/2oz brown breadcrumbs
50g/2oz gruyere cheese, grated
1 egg, beaten
½ tsp chopped fresh sage leaves

Preheat the oven to 180°C/350°F/Gas 4, line a baking sheet with baking parchment and brush the parchment with oil.

Cook the cauliflower and broccoli florets together in a steamer for 5–7 minutes until tender, then remove from the heat and leave to cool.

Put the cooled cauliflower and broccoli in a food processor with the remaining ingredients and blitz until finely chopped. Transfer the mixture to a bowl and shape it into 6 burgers.

Put the burgers on the lined baking sheet and bake in the oven for 15 minutes until firm. Try serving them with my Hidden Treasure Quinoa Salad (see page 70) or Quesadilla with Tomato, Basil and Mozzarella (see page 77).

LENTIL BOLOGNESE

This is spaghetti bolognese but not as you know it. Made with lentils (a great source of protein, iron and fibre) and lots of fantastic veggies, think of this as a super-charged bolognese!

2 tbsp olive oil
1 large red onion, finely chopped
½ red pepper, deseeded and finely diced
2 large garlic cloves, crushed
2 small carrots, finely diced
200g/7oz chestnut mushrooms, diced
50g/2oz dried puy lentils
400g/14oz tin chopped tomatoes
200ml/7fl oz vegetable stock
2 tbsp sun-dried tomato paste
1 tbsp chopped fresh thyme leaves
1 tsp soy sauce
200g/7oz spaghettini or regular spaghetti
salt and pepper

Heat the oil in a saucepan over a medium heat, add the onion, red pepper, garlic, carrots and mushrooms and fry for 5 minutes until softened. Add the lentils and stir to coat them in the mixture, then add the chopped tomatoes, stock and tomato paste and season with a little salt and pepper. Cover, bring to the boil, then reduce the heat and simmer for 25–30 minutes until the lentils are soft and the sauce has reduced. Add the thyme and soy sauce and remove from the heat.

Meanwhile, cook the pasta in a pan of boiling salted water according to the packet instructions, drain, then toss with the sauce and serve.

The sauce can be frozen (once cooled) for up to 2 months. Defrost, then reheat in a saucepan and mix with freshly cooked pasta.

SCRAMBLED EGG MUFFINS

Eggs are a powerhouse of nutrients. Scrambled eggs are quick and super simple to make and this recipe is easy to adapt according to what you have to hand.

knob of butter, plus extra
  for spreading
2 eggs, beaten
2 tbsp milk
3 tbsp grated cheddar cheese
1 English muffin, halved

Melt the butter in a small frying pan over a medium heat. Mix the eggs and milk together in a bowl, then add them to the pan and stir for a minute or so until scrambled. Add the cheese and remove from the heat.

Lightly toast the split muffin, spread both halves with butter and spoon the cheesy scrambled eggs on top.

VARIATIONS
Add sliced spring onion and chopped fresh tomatoes to the pan.

Serve with chopped ham, turkey or smoked salmon cut into strips, wilted spinach and 50g/2oz mushrooms sautéed in a knob of butter and 1 tbsp chopped soft herbs (e.g. chives and basil).

EDAMAME NOODLE SALAD WITH PEANUT DRESSING

Edamame (soya beans) are rich in protein, antioxidants and fibre. Mix them with some colourful veg and toss them with this tasty peanut dressing for a power-packed salad that is suitable for vegans and vegetarians.

125g/4½oz medium egg noodles

125g/4½oz cooked and shelled edamame (soya beans)

4 tbsp tinned sweetcorn

½ red pepper, deseeded and diced

½ apple, peeled and sliced into thin strips

1 small carrot, sliced into thin strips

DRESSING

1 tbsp smooth peanut butter

1 tbsp rice wine vinegar

1 tbsp sweet chilli sauce

2 tsp soy sauce

Cook the noodles in a pan of boiling water according to the packet instructions, drain and rinse under cold running water.

Mix the noodles in a serving bowl with the edamame and remaining ingredients.

Whisk the dressing ingredients together with 2 tablespoons of cold water in a small bowl, then pour the dressing over the salad. Toss together and serve.

CHAPTER 3

15-MINUTE MEALS

JAPANESE-STYLE CHICKEN NOODLE SALAD

Introduce your family to a taste of the orient with this Japanese-inspired noodle salad. It's the perfect opportunity to offer young children new flavour combinations; the simple but standout Japanese dressing will take kids on a taste adventure.

150g/5oz medium egg noodles
198g/7oz tin sweetcorn, drained
1 large carrot, grated
2 large spring onions, sliced
100g/3½oz sugar snap peas, sliced
3 Chinese lettuce leaves, sliced
2 cooked chicken breasts, diced

DRESSING
4 tbsp rice wine vinegar
6 tbsp light olive oil
2 tbsp sweet chilli sauce
1 garlic clove, crushed
2 tbsp soy sauce

Cook the noodles in a pan of boiling water according to the packet instructions, drain and rinse under cold running water. Drain well and tip into a serving bowl.

Add the sweetcorn, carrot, spring onions, sugar snap peas, Chinese lettuce leaves and chicken to the noodles.

Mix all of the dressing ingredients together in a jug. Pour the dressing over the noodle salad, toss together and serve.

INSTANT CHICKEN CURRY

There's no reason why the whole family shouldn't join in on curry nights, especially when the recipe is this quick to prepare! My Instant Chicken Curry is a must-try dish with just the right amount of mild spice and flavour.

200g/7oz cooked chicken
(leftover roast chicken works
well), diced
2 tbsp tinned sweetcorn
25g/1oz frozen peas
cooked rice, to serve

CURRY SAUCE
400g/14oz tin coconut milk
2 tbsp Korma curry paste
1 tbsp mango chutney
½ tsp grated fresh root ginger
75ml/3fl oz chicken stock
a few drops of soy sauce
2 tbsp cornflour
salt and pepper

To make the curry sauce, put the coconut milk, Korma curry paste, mango chutney, ginger, chicken stock and soy sauce in a saucepan over a medium heat. Whisk until simmering.

Mix the cornflour with a little cold water in a small bowl until smooth, then add it to the sauce. Whisk, bring to the boil and cook for about 2 minutes until the sauce has thickened. Season to taste with a little salt and pepper.

Add the chicken, sweetcorn and peas to the sauce and simmer for 3–4 minutes until the peas are cooked. Serve with rice.

TIP

The easiest way to peel ginger is by scraping it with the edge of a teaspoon. If you don't use it all then freeze it and you can use it another time.

Makes 6 portions

CHICKEN AND PESTO BRUSCHETTA

Sweet cherry tomatoes, pesto, grated cheese and diced cooked chicken – a simple match made in heaven to top freshly-baked ciabatta.

½ baked ciabatta loaf, cut into
  6 slices
1 tbsp olive oil
1 tbsp mayonnaise
1 tbsp fresh green pesto
1 tbsp chopped fresh basil leaves
1 cooked chicken breast, diced
6 cherry tomatoes, finely
  chopped
25g/1oz cheddar cheese, grated
salt and pepper

Preheat the oven to 200°C/400°F/Gas 6.

Brush the ciabatta with the olive oil, place on a baking sheet and bake in the oven for 5 minutes until lightly golden.

Combine the remaining ingredients in a small bowl, season lightly with salt and pepper and spoon on top of the slices of bread. Put them back into the oven for about 8 minutes until the topping is warm. Serve immediately.

OMELETTE WITH BROCCOLI, CHERRY TOMATOES AND GRUYERE

Eggs are a real food hero, packed full of nutrients. It's so easy to whip up this quick dish – omelettes are a fantastic solution for a quick breakfast, lunch or light dinner if you find yourself short on time and in need of a quick fix.

50g/2oz broccoli florets
knob of butter
3 spring onions, thinly sliced
2 eggs, beaten
1 tbsp milk
5 cherry tomatoes, quartered
50g/2oz gruyere cheese, grated
salt and pepper

Cook the broccoli florets in a steamer for 3–4 minutes until tender.

Melt the butter in a small frying pan over a medium heat, add the spring onions and fry for 30 seconds. Beat the eggs with the milk, season with a little salt and pepper then pour the eggs into the pan, moving the egg mixture around until the egg starts to set.

Scatter the broccoli, tomatoes and grated cheese over the omelette and cook flat (fold the sides towards the centre over the filling if you prefer) for a further 3–4 minutes until the omelette is set but has a slight wobble.

THE BEST BUTTERMILK PANCAKES

Pancakes always go down an absolute treat and it's incredibly quick and easy to cook up a batch. For the very best buttermilk pancakes, use a ladle so that the mixture goes into the pan all in one go, then simply tilt the pan to make a regular and even circle. *Et voilà* – perfect pancakes.

175g/6oz self-raising flour
½ tsp bicarbonate of soda
pinch of fine salt
20g/¾oz caster sugar
1 egg, beaten
150ml/5fl oz buttermilk
150ml/5fl oz whole milk
40g/1½oz butter, melted
1–2 tbsp sunflower oil
fresh berries, yoghurt and maple
    syrup, to serve (or topping of
    choice)

Preheat the oven to 180°C/350°F/Gas 4.

Combine the flour, bicarbonate of soda, salt and sugar in a bowl. Whisk the egg, buttermilk, milk and melted butter together in a separate bowl. Gently and gradually whisk the wet ingredients into the dry ingredients until the batter is smooth and lump free.

Heat 1 tablespoon of the oil in a large frying pan over a medium heat. Spoon two large spoonfuls (or, even better, a ladleful) of the pancake batter into the pan to make a large pancake, tilt the pan to give the pancake an even thickness, and fry for 2–3 minutes, then carefully flip the pancake over and cook for a further 2 minutes until lightly golden and cooked through.

Repeat three times with the remaining mixture, adding more oil to the pan if necessary, to make 4 large pancakes. Keep the cooked pancakes warm on a baking sheet (uncovered) in the oven.

Serve with fresh berries, natural yoghurt and maple syrup, or your topping of choice.

The cooked pancakes can be frozen between layers of greaseproof paper and reheated in the oven or microwave.

TORTILLA PIZZAS

The word 'pizza' immediately elicits children's excitement come dinnertime. My tortilla pizzas are not only guaranteed to result in clean plates but they are a great way to get your mini chefs helping out in the kitchen: children like to assemble their own food, so try putting the ingredients in bowls and let them top their very own pizza. It's amazing how being involved in the preparation of a meal can stimulate a child's appetite.

olive oil, for greasing
2 large tortilla wraps
6 tbsp tinned chopped tomatoes
2 tbsp fresh or jarred red pesto
1 tbsp chopped fresh basil leaves
40g/1½oz mozzarella, cubed
40g/1½oz cooked chicken, sliced
2 tbsp tinned sweetcorn
4 tbsp grated parmesan cheese

Preheat the grill to high and grease a baking sheet.

Put the tortilla wraps on the baking sheet.

Mix the chopped tomatoes and pesto together in a bowl then spread the mixture over each tortilla.

Divide the basil, mozzarella, chicken, sweetcorn and parmesan evenly between each tortilla and grill them for 5 minutes until golden and crisp.

PITTA BREAD TORTILLA CHIPS WITH TOMATO SALSA

Chips and dip is a firm family favourite and it's so simple to make your own. Cook up a batch of tortilla chips, pop on your favourite family film, curl up on the sofa and get dipping!

3 pitta breads
3 tbsp olive oil
1 small garlic clove, crushed
½ tsp chopped fresh thyme leaves

SALSA
150g/5oz cherry tomatoes, finely chopped
1 tbsp chopped fresh basil leaves
20g/¾oz cheddar cheese, grated

Preheat the grill to high.

Slice the pitta breads in half through the middle so you have 6 slices of pitta, then slice each half into triangles.

Mix the oil, garlic and thyme leaves together in a bowl. Brush the mixture over the pitta triangles on both sides and arrange the triangles on a baking sheet. Put the pitta triangles under the grill for about 8 minutes, turning them over halfway through, until lightly golden and crisp.

Transfer the grilled tortilla chips to a shallow ovenproof dish.

Mix the salsa ingredients together in the bowl with any remaining garlic, oil and thyme and spoon it over the chips. Top with the grated cheese and put back under the grill for 3–4 minutes until melted.

BUTTERNUT SQUASH CARBONARA

Dig in your fork, twirl around the spaghetti and tuck into this deliciously rich and meatless creamy carbonara.

2 tbsp olive oil
1 small onion, finely diced
150g/5oz butternut squash,
  peeled and diced
2 garlic cloves, crushed
2 tbsp chopped fresh thyme
  leaves
100g/3½oz spaghettini or regular
  spaghetti
2 eggs, beaten
100g/3½oz parmesan cheese,
  grated
salt and pepper

Heat the oil in a frying pan over a medium heat, add the onion and fry for 2 minutes until softened, then add the squash and cook for 8–10 minutes until lightly golden and soft. Add the garlic and thyme and fry for 30 seconds.

While the squash is cooking, cook the pasta in a pan of boiling salted water according to the packet instructions, drain then add it straight into the frying pan after the garlic and thyme.

Mix half the grated cheese into the beaten eggs. Add the egg mixture to the pasta in the pan and remove the pan from the heat. Stir well and season with a little salt and pepper.

Sprinkle with the remaining cheese, toss together and serve straight away.

CHICKEN AND VEGETABLE PASTA

There's no easier way to your family's five-a-day than this chicken and vegetable pasta dish with a deliciously light, quick and easy cheese sauce made with crème fraîche, stock, parmesan and a squeeze of lemon.

200g/7oz small bow-tie pasta
  (farfalle)
50g/2oz frozen peas
2 tbsp olive oil
2 skinless chicken breasts, diced
1 onion, finely chopped
½ red pepper, deseeded and diced
1 medium courgette, thinly sliced
1 garlic clove, crushed
100ml/3½fl oz chicken stock
150g/5oz crème fraîche
squeeze of lemon juice
50g/2oz parmesan cheese, grated
small bunch of fresh basil,
  chopped
salt and pepper

Cook the pasta in a pan of boiling salted water according to the packet instructions, adding the peas 4 minutes before the end of the cooking time, then drain.

While the pasta is cooking, heat 1 tablespoon of the oil in a frying pan over a high heat, season the chicken lightly with salt and pepper and fry for 3–4 minutes until golden and cooked through. Transfer to a plate and set aside.

Heat the remaining oil in a frying pan (you can use the same pan you fried the chicken in) over a medium heat. Add the onion, red pepper and courgette and fry for 3–4 minutes until softened, then add the garlic and cook for about 30 seconds. Add the chicken stock, bring to the boil and cook until reduced by half.

Add the crème fraîche, pasta and peas, chicken and lemon juice. Increase the heat to high and toss together. Season lightly with salt and pepper, remove from the heat and add the parmesan and basil. Stir together and serve.

PRAWN PATTIES

This is my oriental twist on the traditional fishcake. With garlic, ginger and spring onions, the patties are full of flavour and ideal for younger members of the family who are new to prawns or perhaps yet to be convinced of their deliciousness.

½ red pepper, deseeded and diced

4 spring onions, chopped

½ tsp grated fresh root ginger

1 garlic clove, crushed

2 tbsp tinned sweetcorn

300g/11oz raw shelled prawns

55g/2oz panko or dried
   breadcrumbs

2 tbsp sunflower oil

Put the red pepper, spring onions, ginger, garlic and sweetcorn in a food processor and blitz until roughly chopped. Add the prawns and 20g/¾oz of the panko breadcrumbs and blitz again until the mixture is finely chopped.

Transfer the mixture to a bowl and shape it into 6 patties. Put the rest of the breadcrumbs in a shallow bowl and use them to coat each patty.

Heat the oil in a frying pan over a medium heat, add the patties and fry for 5–8 minutes, carefully turning them once, until golden and cooked through. Remove from the heat and drain on kitchen paper.

The cooked patties can be frozen (once cooled) for up to 2 months. Defrost, then reheat in a preheated oven at 180°C/350°F/Gas 4 for about 20 minutes, or in the microwave, until warmed through.

SEA BASS WITH A QUICK CHERRY TOMATO SAUCE

A quick simple sauce is all you need to serve alongside this beautiful fish. It's perfect for a short-on-time supper but equally suitable for a special occasion.

---

2 sea bass fillets, halved
  lengthways
4 tbsp plain flour
1 tbsp olive oil
knob of butter
salt and pepper

CHERRY TOMATO SAUCE
2 tbsp olive oil
1 small red onion, finely diced
1 garlic clove, crushed
300g/11oz cherry tomatoes,
  quartered
1 tbsp good-quality balsamic
  vinegar
pinch of sugar
2 tbsp thinly sliced fresh
  basil leaves

Season the sea bass pieces with a little salt and pepper and coat them with flour on both sides.

Heat the oil and butter in a frying pan over a medium heat. When the butter has melted and starts to foam, add the floured sea bass and fry for 2 minutes on each side until lightly golden and cooked through. Remove from the pan and set aside.

To make the sauce, heat the olive oil in a separate frying pan over a medium heat, add the onion and fry for 3–4 minutes, then add the garlic and cook for 30 seconds. Add the tomatoes and fry for 2 minutes, until they start to soften, then add the balsamic vinegar, sugar and basil and cook for 1 minute. Season with a little salt and pepper.

Spoon the quick cherry tomato sauce over the fish and serve.

Makes 3 portions

SIMPLE SALMON WITH PLUM AND SOY SAUCE

Oily fish like salmon aids brain development and children should aim to have two portions of oily fish a week for a boost of omega 3s. This is a quick, easy and delicious recipe that everyone can enjoy. Serve with rice or noodles along with your favourite steamed or stir-fried veggies.

sunflower oil, for greasing
1 tbsp plum sauce
2 tsp soy sauce
2 tsp orange juice
300g/11oz skinless salmon fillet, cut into 2cm/¾in chunks
cooked vegetables of choice, to serve
cooked rice or noodles, to serve

Preheat the grill to high, line a baking sheet with foil and lightly grease it with oil.

Mix the plum sauce, soy sauce and orange juice together in a bowl, add the salmon chunks and leave to marinate for 5 minutes.

Place the salmon chunks on the lined baking sheet and put under the grill for 5 minutes, until the salmon is cooked through and lightly golden.

Serve with cooked vegetables, such as peas and steamed baby carrots, and rice or noodles.

QUICK PRAWN AND BROCCOLI STIR-FRY

I love this simple prawn stir-fry. The secret to making it extra delicious is to keep the broccoli crisp and crunchy.

1 tbsp sunflower oil
1 onion, finely chopped
1 garlic clove, crushed
1 tsp freshly grated root ginger
275ml/9fl oz chicken stock
1 tbsp cornflour
1 tsp soy sauce
2 tsp sweet chilli sauce
2 spring onions, thinly sliced
100g/3½oz broccoli florets
250g/9oz jumbo cooked
 peeled prawns
cooked rice, to serve

Heat the oil in a saucepan over a medium heat, add the onion and fry for 3–4 minutes until softened, then add the garlic and ginger and fry for 30 seconds. Add the stock and bring to the boil.

Mix the cornflour in a small bowl with 4 tablespoons of cold water, then add it to the hot stock and stir over the heat for about 2 minutes until thickened. Stir in the soy sauce, sweet chilli sauce and spring onions and cook for a minute, then add the broccoli and simmer for 2 minutes. Add the prawns and cook for a further 2–3 minutes until the prawns are heated through but the broccoli still has a crunchy texture.

Serve with rice.

VARIATION
Quick Chicken and Sugar Snap Pea Stir-Fry
After frying the onion, garlic and ginger add 250g/9oz chicken breast cut into strips and fry for around 4 minutes. Swap the broccoli for 100g/3½oz sugar snap peas.

TERIYAKI BEEF STIR-FRY

Stir-fries are quick, easy and flexible, too: you can mix and match ingredients depending on what you have to hand. Try using chicken instead of the steak, or a different selection of vegetables. What gives it that magical child appeal is the tasty marinade made with rice wine vinegar and mirin, which can now be found in most supermarkets.

300g/11oz sirloin steak, trimmed
150g/5oz medium egg noodles
2 tbsp sunflower oil
½ large onion, sliced
1 red pepper, deseeded and diced
150g/5oz button mushrooms,
   sliced
1 medium courgette, sliced into
   batons
1 tsp grated fresh root ginger
1 garlic clove, crushed
handful of beansprouts
salt and pepper
spring onions, chopped,
   to garnish (optional)

MARINADE
4 tbsp soy sauce
2 tbsp soft light brown sugar
2 tbsp rice wine vinegar
2 tsp sesame oil
1 tbsp mirin

Mix all of the marinade ingredients together in a bowl.

Put the steak on a chopping board and cover it with a piece of clingfilm. Bash it with a meat mallet or similar heavy weight to make it thinner, then remove the clingfilm and slice it into thin strips. Add the strips to the marinade, stir to coat and leave to marinate for 5 minutes while you cook the noodles.

Cook the noodles in a pan of boiling water according to the packet instructions, then drain.

Heat 1 tablespoon of the sunflower oil in a wok or large frying pan, drain the beef (reserving the marinade) and add it to the wok. Fry for 1 minute, then transfer to a plate.

Wipe the wok or frying pan clean and add the remaining oil. Add the onion, red pepper, mushrooms and courgette to the wok and stir-fry for 2–3 minutes. Stir the ginger and garlic into the reserved marinade and add it to the wok or frying pan. Bring to the boil, then add the cooked noodles. Toss over the heat and season lightly with salt and pepper. Finally, add the beef and beansprouts, remove from the heat and serve, with spring onions to garnish (if you like).

PRAWN SALAD BOATS

For a quick and easy light lunch, these lettuce boats are a more interesting alternative to sandwiches. Simply load up your lettuce leaves and that's it – you are good to go!

2 tbsp mayonnaise
1 tbsp sweet chilli sauce
squeeze of lemon juice
150g/5oz jumbo cooked and peeled prawns, finely chopped
3 tbsp tinned sweetcorn
¼ cucumber, deseeded and diced
5 cherry tomatoes, quartered
4 spring onions, thinly sliced
150g/5oz cooked long grain rice (cold)
½ apple, peeled and diced
12 leaves from 1 large gem lettuce
salt and pepper

Put all of the ingredients (except the lettuce) in a bowl. Season lightly with salt and pepper and mix to combine.

Arrange the lettuce leaves on a serving plate and spoon some prawn salad into each lettuce 'boat'.

TIP

Microwave a lemon for just 15 seconds and you will double the juice you get from squeezing.

FRESH TOMATO SPAGHETTINI

There is nothing more satisfying than making your own tasty tomato sauce and it really is so simple. It's great as a base for a homemade pizza or here, simply stirred into spaghettini or spaghetti.

3 tbsp olive oil
2 banana shallots, finely diced
2 garlic cloves, crushed
350g/12oz ripe cherry tomatoes, finely chopped
2 tbsp rice wine vinegar
knob of butter
225g/8oz spaghettini or regular spaghetti
20g/¾oz parmesan cheese, finely grated
small bunch of basil, leaves chopped
salt and pepper

Heat the oil in a frying pan over a medium heat, add the shallots and fry for a few minutes until softened, then add the garlic and fry for 30 seconds. Remove from the heat and stir in the tomatoes, vinegar and butter.

Cook the pasta in a pan of boiling salted water according to the packet instructions, drain and add straight to the sauce in the frying pan so there is still some pasta water clinging to the pasta.

Add the parmesan and basil, toss together in the pan, season with a little salt and pepper and serve straight away.

ALPHABET SOUP

My Alphabet Soup really is as easy as ABC.

knob of butter
1 tbsp sunflower oil
1 onion, finely chopped
100g/3½oz carrot, diced
75g/3oz butternut squash, peeled
   and diced
2 tbsp plain flour
900ml/30fl oz chicken stock
300g/11oz frozen garden peas
100g/3½oz cooked chicken, diced
50g/2oz alphabet pasta
salt

Melt the butter with the oil in a saucepan over a medium heat, add the onion, carrot and squash and fry for 3–4 minutes, then sprinkle in the flour and stir for 10 seconds. Gradually add the stock, stirring until the soup thickens and reaches boiling point, then reduce the heat and simmer for 10 minutes. Add the chicken and peas and cook for about 3 minutes, or until the peas are cooked.

Cook the pasta in a pan of boiling salted water according to the packet instructions, then drain, add it to the soup and serve.

The soup can be frozen (once cooled) for up to 3 months. Freeze it on portions, defrost, then reheat in a pan for about 5 minutes until heated through.

GRILLED CHICKEN BURGERS

I think it's important to try and make your own alternative healthy versions of fast food: burgers needn't be seen as an unhealthy meal option. My Grilled Chicken Burgers are flavoured with tomato chutney, packed full of protein, contain hidden grated carrot and are grilled rather than fried for a guilt-free family favourite.

50g/2oz fresh white breadcrumbs
1 red onion, finely chopped
1 garlic clove, crushed
250g/9oz minced chicken
2 tsp soy sauce
3 tbsp tomato chutney
50g/2oz carrot, grated
sunflower oil, for greasing
salt and pepper
cooked vegetables, to serve

Preheat the grill to high.

Put all the ingredients (except the oil) in a food processor and blitz until finely chopped and well combined. Transfer the mixture to a bowl and season lightly with salt and pepper.

Shape the mixture into 10 burgers and flatten them slightly.

Line a baking tray with foil and grease the foil with oil. Place the burgers on the tray and cook under the hot grill for 6–7 minutes each side until lightly golden and cooked through.

Serve with vegetables such as broccoli and corn on the cob.

The cooked burgers can be frozen (once cooled) for up to 2 months. Defrost, then reheat in the oven at 180°C/350°F/Gas 4 for 10–12 minutes, or until heated through.

CHAPTER 4

HEALTHY 'FAST' FOOD

YUMMY CHICKEN QUESADILLA

This is the ultimate quesadilla combo. The chicken is so full of flavour from the mouthwatering marinade of soy sauce, garlic and maple syrup that it's simply too good to resist.

1 garlic clove, crushed

1 tsp maple syrup

1 tsp soy sauce

1 skinless chicken breast, thinly sliced

1 tbsp sunflower oil

½ red pepper, deseeded and diced

3 tbsp tinned sweetcorn

4 spring onions, sliced

4 corn tortillas

2 tbsp sun-dried tomato paste

2 tbsp mayonnaise

50g/2oz cheddar cheese, grated

Mix the garlic, maple syrup and soy sauce in a bowl, add the sliced chicken and leave to marinate for 5 minutes.

Heat the oil in a large frying pan over a medium heat, add the chicken and fry until cooked through, then transfer it to a bowl. Add the pepper, sweetcorn and spring onions to the frying pan and fry for 2–3 minutes, then add the mixture to the chicken in the bowl. Remove the pan from the heat and wipe it clean.

Put 2 of the tortillas on a board. Spread them both with tomato paste and mayonnaise. Top with the chicken mixture and cheese. Place the other 2 wraps on top of the filling and press down.

Put the pan back over the heat and fry the quesadillas, one at a time, for 2–3 minutes on each side, until golden on both sides and the cheese in the filling has melted. Remove from the pan and slice each quesadilla into 6 wedges. Serve straight away.

BAKED CHICKEN WRAPS

Filled with protein-packed chicken, colourful veggies and oozy melted cheese, these baked wraps will soon become flavoursome favourites. They are a great way to use up leftover roast chicken, too.

1 tbsp olive oil, plus extra
    for greasing
½ red onion, finely chopped
½ red pepper, deseeded
    and diced
½ courgette, diced
1 garlic clove, crushed
200g/7oz tinned chopped
    tomatoes
1 tbsp tomato puree
1 tsp honey
2 tbsp chopped fresh
    basil leaves
100g/3½oz cooked chicken,
    diced
50g/2oz cheddar cheese, grated
6 mini tortillas
salt and pepper

Preheat the grill to high and grease a small-medium ovenproof dish with oil.

Heat the oil in a saucepan over a medium heat, add the onion, red pepper, courgette and garlic and fry for 5 minutes, then add the chopped tomatoes, tomato puree and honey and simmer for 5 minutes. Add the basil and chicken and season lightly with salt and pepper.

Divide the filling between the 6 wraps and top with half the grated cheese. Roll them up and place them in the oiled ovenproof dish. Brush the wraps with a little oil and sprinkle with the remaining cheese.

Place under the hot grill for 15 minutes until lightly golden and crisp.

CHICKEN CHOW MEIN

Sweet, succulent and packed full of colourful veggies, this is the perfect midweek meal for growing families. And who doesn't love to slurp their way through a bowl of noodles?

125g/4½oz medium egg
 noodles
2 skinless chicken breasts,
 thinly sliced
1 tbsp sweet chilli sauce
2 tbsp sunflower oil
1 onion, thinly sliced
½ yellow pepper, deseeded
 and thinly sliced
1 carrot, sliced lengthways
 into thin strips
175g/6oz baby corn, cut
 lengthways into quarters
100g/3½oz brown mushrooms,
 thinly sliced
¼ savoy cabbage, thinly sliced
salt and pepper

SAUCE
1 tsp grated fresh root ginger
2 tbsp soy sauce
2 tbsp dry sherry
1 tbsp sweet chilli sauce

Cook the noodles in a pan of boiling water according to the packet instructions, drain and refresh under cold running water.

Season the chicken slices with a little salt and pepper and add the tablespoon of chilli sauce.

Heat half the sunflower oil in a wok or large frying pan over a high heat, add the chicken and fry for about 4 minutes until cooked and lightly golden, then transfer the chicken to a plate or bowl.

Heat the remaining oil in the wok, add the onion, pepper, carrot and baby corn and stir-fry over a high heat for 3 minutes, then add the mushrooms and cabbage and fry for a further 2 minutes. Add the cooked noodles to the wok.

Mix all of the sauce ingredients together in a small bowl, then pour it over the vegetables and chicken and toss together. Serve straight away.

FINGER LICKIN' CHICKEN WINGS

Finger lickin' is a bold claim but it's absolutely warranted on this occasion. The thick, stick and sweet Chinese-style glaze is so good it's worth getting a bit messy for! Get napkins at the ready ...

1kg/2¼lb chicken wings

CHINESE SAUCE
1 tbsp white wine vinegar
2 tbsp soy sauce
1 tbsp soft light brown sugar
½ tsp grated fresh root ginger
2 tbsp sweet chilli sauce, plus
  extra to serve
4 tbsp tomato ketchup
½ tsp Chinese five-spice

Preheat the oven to 180°C/350°F/Gas 4 and line a baking tray or roasting tin with baking parchment.

Mix the sauce ingredients in a large bowl, add the chicken wings and mix well to coat them with the sauce, then transfer them to the baking tray or roasting tin and spread them out evenly.

Let them marinate in the mixture for 10 minutes, then bake in the oven for 30–35 minutes, turning the wings over halfway through the cooking time, until golden and cooked through.

Serve with extra chilli sauce on the side, for dipping.

CHINESE-STYLE PORK CROQUETTES

Introduce your children to a taste of oriental food with my Chinese-style croquettes. Serve them on their own as a finger-food favourite or team with stir-fried veggies for a complete meal. If you prefer, you can make the croquettes with minced chicken instead of pork.

3 tbsp sunflower oil

4–5 spring onions, thinly sliced

75g/3oz carrot, finely diced

175g/6oz minced pork

1 garlic clove, crushed

1 tbsp soy sauce

1 tbsp mirin

1 tbsp plum sauce

200g/7oz cooked mashed potatoes, cooled

COATING

1 tbsp plain flour

1 egg, beaten

30g/1¼oz panko or dried breadcrumbs

Heat 1 tablespoon of the oil in a frying pan over a medium heat, add the onions and carrot and fry for 2–3 minutes until softened. Add the pork and fry for about 4 minutes until browned, breaking up the mince with a wooden spoon. Add the garlic, soy sauce, mirin and plum sauce and fry for a further 2 minutes. Transfer to a bowl and leave to cool.

Once cold, mix the potato into the pork mixture, then mould the mixture into 10 croquette shapes.

Put the flour for the coating in a bowl, the beaten egg in another bowl and the breadcrumbs in a third bowl. Coat each croquette in the flour, then the egg, then the breadcrumbs.

Heat the remaining oil in a large frying pan over a medium heat, add the croquettes and fry for 5–8 minutes until golden and heated through, turning them so they cook evenly.

The cooked croquettes can be frozen (once cooled) for up to 2 months. Defrost, then reheat in the oven at 180°C/350°F/Gas 4 for about 10 minutes, or until heated through.

PULLED CHICKEN BAPS WITH APPLE COLESLAW

A lovely combination of simple glazed chicken shredded with forks and served on top of crunchy coleslaw in a brioche bun.

2 skinless chicken breasts

4 small brioche buns

salt and pepper

soft lettuce leaves and sliced
  tomato, to serve

sweet potato wedges, to serve
  (see page 67)

GLAZE

1 tsp soft light brown sugar

1 tsp soy sauce

½ tsp grated fresh root ginger

2 tbsp tomato ketchup

APPLE COLESLAW

100g/3½oz red cabbage,
  shredded

2 spring onions, sliced

1 medium carrot, peeled
  and grated

½ apple, peeled and grated

2 tbsp mayonnaise

squeeze of lemon juice

Preheat the oven to 180°C/350°F/Gas 4 and line a baking tray with baking parchment.

Put the chicken breasts on the baking sheet and season lightly with salt and pepper. Combine the glaze ingredients and spread the glaze over the top of the breasts. Bake them in the oven for 18–20 minutes, or until cooked through. Remove from the oven and leave to cool slightly on the tray, then pull apart the breasts using forks and shred the meat.

Mix all of the coleslaw ingredients together in a bowl and season lightly with salt and pepper.

Slice a brioche bun in half. Put a lettuce leaf on the bottom half with a slice of tomato, then some coleslaw, followed by some pulled chicken. Cover with the other half of the bun, fill the remaining brioche buns and serve with sweet potato wedges.

CHICKEN WITH MOZZARELLA, CHERRY TOMATOES AND BASIL

Tender chicken breasts topped with a tasty tomato sauce with melted mozzarella, fresh basil and cherry tomatoes. Serve with the crispy roasted herb potatoes.

---

2 skinless chicken breasts, each cut into 3 pieces
50g/2oz plain flour
2 eggs, beaten
75g/3oz panko or dried breadcrumbs
2 tbsp sunflower oil
100g/3½oz cherry tomatoes, halved
10 mini mozzarella balls
salt and pepper

ROASTED HERB POTATOES
350g/12oz peeled potatoes, cut into small dice
2 tbsp sunflower oil
1 tsp chopped fresh thyme leaves

TOMATO SAUCE
1 tbsp olive oil
1 onion, finely chopped
2 garlic cloves, crushed
400g/14oz tin chopped tomatoes
1 tbsp sun-dried tomato paste
pinch of sugar
2 tbsp chopped fresh basil leaves

Preheat the oven to 200°C/400°F/Gas 6.

Put the potatoes and oil in a small roasting tin. Toss together and season lightly with salt and pepper. Roast in the oven for 30 minutes until golden and crispy, adding the thyme and tossing them after 20 minutes.

Meanwhile, make the tomato sauce. Heat the oil in a saucepan over a medium heat, add the onion and fry for 3 minutes until softened, then add the garlic and fry for 30 seconds. Add the chopped tomatoes, tomato paste and sugar, cover and bring to the boil, then reduce the heat and simmer for 10 minutes.

Put the chicken pieces on a chopping board, cover with clingfilm then bash with a meat mallet or other heavy object until thin. Remove the clingfilm and season lightly with salt and pepper. Put the flour in a bowl, the beaten eggs in another bowl and the breadcrumbs in a third bowl. Coat each chicken strip in flour, then the egg, then the breadcrumbs. Heat the oil in a frying pan over a medium heat, add the coated chicken pieces and fry for 2 minutes on each side until golden and nearly cooked through. Preheat the grill to high.

Stir the basil into the tomato sauce and spread it out in a shallow ovenproof dish. Put the chicken pieces on top and scatter over the cherry tomatoes and mozzarella balls. Grill for 5–8 minutes until bubbling and serve.

MINI CHICKEN BURGERS WITH APPLE AND SAGE

This is a more grown-up twist on my signature Chicken and Apple Balls recipe from my *New Complete Baby and Toddler Meal Planner*. The grated apple and sage add an irresistible sweetness and depth of flavour to these mini burgers.

350g/12oz chicken thigh
  fillets, chopped
50g/2oz fresh white
  breadcrumbs
85g/3¼oz onion, diced
70g/2¾oz celery, diced
25g/1oz deseeded red pepper,
  diced
50g/2oz peeled and grated
  apple
2 tsp soy sauce
2 tbsp fresh chopped sage
  leaves
sunflower oil, for frying
roasted sweet potato wedges (see
  page 67), cooked broccoli or
  baby carrots, to serve

Put the chicken in a food processor and blitz until finely chopped. Add the remaining ingredients and pulse until the mixture comes together. Transfer the mixture to a bowl and shape it into 20 mini burgers with your hands.

Heat a drizzle of oil in a large frying pan over a high heat, add 10 of the burgers and fry for 2–3 minutes on each side until golden and cooked through. Transfer to kitchen paper to absorb excess oil, then cook the remaining 10 burgers in the same way. Serve with roasted sweet potato wedges or broccoli and carrots.

The burgers can be frozen (once cooled) for up to 2 months. Defrost, then reheat in a preheated oven at 180°C/350°F/ Gas 4 for about 20 minutes, or until heated through.

SWEET AND SOUR CHICKEN

Here's a Chinese takeaway favourite that the whole family can enjoy at home. The twist? My recipe is both healthy and super tasty! With succulent chicken and a special sweet 'n' sour sauce, it's so tasty children are bound to lap up all the veggies too. Clean plates all round.

75g/3oz butternut squash, peeled and diced
100g/3½oz broccoli florets
75g/3oz baby corn
1 egg yolk
1 tbsp milk
2 tbsp cornflour
2 skinless chicken breasts, diced
2 tbsp sunflower oil
4 spring onions, sliced
salt and pepper
cooked rice, to serve

SWEET AND SOUR SAUCE
1 tbsp soy sauce
2 tbsp tomato ketchup
2 tbsp rice wine vinegar
½–1 tbsp maple syrup
50ml/2fl oz water
1 tsp cornflour
2 tbsp apple juice

Steam the diced butternut squash in a steamer for 5 minutes, then add the broccoli and baby corn and steam for a further 4 minutes until the vegetables are tender.

Beat the egg yolk, milk and cornflour together in a bowl. Add the diced chicken, lightly season with salt and pepper and stir to coat the chicken in the batter.

Combine the sweet and sour sauce ingredients in a bowl.

Heat the sunflower oil in a wok or large frying pan over a high heat. Add the chicken and fry for 1–2 minutes until it is golden brown on one side, then cook on the other side for 2 minutes until browned all over. Add the spring onions and fry for about 2 minutes until slightly softened and the chicken is cooked through. Add the sauce and bring to the boil, then add the steamed vegetables and taste to check the seasoning, adding more salt and pepper if you wish.

Serve with rice. I like to make mounds of rice on plates using an ice cream scoop or filling then upturning a ramekin.

The chicken (without the rice) can be frozen (once cooled) for up to 2 months. Defrost, then reheat in the oven at 180°C/350°F/Gas 4 for about 20 minutes, or until heated through.

Makes 4 portions

QUINOA BAKED CHICKEN FINGERS

My healthy chicken nuggets! These are tossed in sun-dried tomato paste, coated in quinoa, parmesan and fresh thyme and baked in the oven until golden.

150g/5oz cooked red and white quinoa, cooled
1 tsp chopped fresh thyme leaves
25g/1oz parmesan cheese, grated
350g/12oz small chicken breast fillets
2 tbsp sun-dried tomato paste
salt and pepper
cooked carrot batons and peas, to serve
ketchup, to serve

Preheat the oven to 180°C/350°F/Gas 4 and line a baking sheet with baking parchment.

Mix the quinoa, thyme and cheese in a bowl with a little salt and pepper.

Put the chicken and sun-dried tomato paste in a bowl. Toss to coat the chicken in the paste, then coat each piece of chicken in the quinoa mixture, patting it onto the chicken so it sticks. Arrange the coated chicken pieces on the lined baking sheet.

Bake in the oven for 15–18 minutes until golden and cooked through.

Serve with carrot batons and peas.

CHICKEN, HALLOUMI AND VEGETABLE KEBABS

Halloumi has a high melting point which means it keeps its shape nicely when cooked. It might seem simple but threading bite-sized pieces of food onto skewers gives food instant child appeal. They look fun and kids will also feel like they have their very own special mini portion. Just remember to remove the skewers before serving to younger children.

200g/7oz skinless chicken breast, cubed
1 tbsp sweet chilli sauce
1 tsp soy sauce
½ large courgette, halved lengthways and sliced into 2cm/¾in-thick crescents
½ large red pepper, deseeded and cut into 2cm/¾in chunks
100g/3½oz halloumi cheese, cut into 2cm/¾in cubes
2 tbsp sunflower oil
salt and pepper

TIP

When using wooden skewers for kebabs, soak them in cold water for 10–30 minutes to prevent them from burning. If using metal skewers, choose square or twisted skewers as food tends to fall off round skewers.

Put the cubed chicken, sweet chilli sauce and soy sauce in a bowl, mix to coat and leave to marinate for 30 minutes.

If you're using wooden skewers, soak them in water before using (see Tip).

Thread a piece of courgette, marinated chicken, red pepper and halloumi cheese onto a skewer and repeat twice so you have three pieces of everything on the skewer. Repeat with the remaining skewers. Season lightly with salt and pepper.

Heat the oil in a large flat frying pan or griddle pan over a high heat. Add the skewers, reduce the heat to medium and fry for about 5 minutes on each side until golden and the chicken is cooked through (you may need to hold the skewers down onto the surface of the frying pan to help them cook through – I place a separate heavy frying pan on top of the skewers to hold them down).

Serve straight away.

THAI CHICKEN AND RICE SOUP

This soup is a meal in itself, with tender chunks of chicken and rice flavoured with Thai curry paste, lemongrass and lime. It's a big favourite in my house.

1 tbsp sunflower oil

1 onion, finely chopped

1 garlic clove, crushed

1 tsp grated fresh root ginger

2½ tbsp red Thai curry paste

2 x 400g/14oz tins coconut milk

350ml/12fl oz chicken stock

1 lemongrass stalk, bashed

2 tsp runny honey

2 tsp fish sauce

grated zest and juice of ½ lime

100g/3½oz button mushrooms, thinly sliced

150g/5oz cooked chicken breast, diced

100g/3½oz long grain rice

Heat the oil in a saucepan over a medium heat, add the onion, garlic and ginger and fry for 2 minutes, then add the curry paste and fry for 10 seconds. Add the coconut milk, chicken stock, lemongrass, honey, fish sauce and lime zest and juice. Bring to the boil, then reduce the heat and simmer for 5 minutes. Add the mushrooms and chicken and simmer for a further 5 minutes.

Meanwhile, cook the rice in a pan of boiling water according to the packet instructions, then drain and stir into the soup before removing the lemongrass stalk and serving.

The soup can be frozen (once cooled) for up to 2 months. Defrost, then reheat in a saucepan or microwave until piping hot.

ANNABEL'S CHICKEN PAD THAI

Pad Thai is a takeaway classic and this is one of my go-to favourites. Not only is this a healthier version, it's a great dish to help introduce younger family members to new flavour combinations.

---

2 skinless chicken breasts, sliced into thin strips
1 tbsp soy sauce
1 tbsp honey
200g/7oz medium rice noodles
150g/5oz broccoli florets
2 tbsp sunflower oil, plus 1 tsp
1 large shallot, thinly sliced, plus extra to fry at the end (optional)
1 large carrot, sliced into batons
1 garlic clove, crushed
½ red chilli, thinly sliced, plus extra to serve (optional)
4 spring onions, thinly sliced
200g/7oz beansprouts
100g/3½oz unsalted roasted peanuts, chopped, plus extra to serve (optional)
2 eggs, beaten
lime wedges, to serve (optional)
salt and pepper

SAUCE
1 tbsp white wine vinegar
2 tbsp soy sauce
1 tbsp fish sauce
2 tbsp sweet chilli sauce

Put the chicken strips in a bowl with the soy sauce and honey and season lightly with salt and pepper. Cook the noodles in a pan of boiling water according to the packet instructions, then drain.

In the meantime, steam or boil the broccoli florets in a separate pan for 3–4 minutes, then drain.

Heat the 2 tablespoons of oil in a wok or large frying pan over a high heat. Add the chicken and stir-fry for about 4 minutes until browned all over and cooked through. Transfer the chicken to a bowl or plate and set aside.

With the wok or frying pan back over the heat, add the shallot, carrot, garlic and chilli (if using) and fry for 3 minutes, then add the drained noodles and broccoli and the spring onions.

Mix the sauce ingredients together in a bowl, pour it over the noodles and toss together. Add the chicken and beansprouts and fry for 1 minute, then spoon into a serving bowl and sprinkle with the peanuts.

Wipe the wok or frying pan clean with kitchen paper, and put it back over a high heat with the teaspoon of oil. Add the beaten eggs and cook, stirring, until scrambled, then spoon on top of the pad Thai and serve straight away, with extra peanuts, chilli, lime wedges and some crispy fried shallot, if you like.

COD AND PRAWN BALLS WITH CHINESE DIPPING SAUCE

These oriental cod and prawn balls are delicious dunked in my Chinese dipping sauce for an added sweet and spicy hit.

150g/5oz skinless cod fillet, diced
150g/5oz raw shelled prawns
1 tsp grated fresh root ginger
1 garlic clove, crushed
1 tbsp sweet chilli sauce
½ tsp fish sauce
60g/2¼oz panko or dried breadcrumbs
2 tbsp sunflower oil
salt and pepper

DIPPING SAUCE
300ml/10fl oz vegetable or chicken stock
2 tsp soy sauce
1 tsp sesame oil
1 tsp sweet chilli sauce
1 tbsp caster sugar
1 tsp rice wine vinegar
1 tbsp cornflour
1 spring onion, thinly sliced

Put the cod, prawns, ginger, garlic, sweet chilli sauce, fish sauce and half the panko breadcrumbs in a food processor and blitz until finely chopped.

Transfer the mixture to a bowl, season with a little salt and pepper and shape it into 12 balls, then roll each ball in the remaining breadcrumbs.

Mix all of the sauce ingredients in a small saucepan, bring to the boil, then reduce the heat and simmer for about 2 minutes until thickened.

Heat the oil in a large frying pan over a medium heat, add the balls and fry for 8–10 minutes until golden and cooked through. Serve them with the warm dipping sauce.

The raw balls can be frozen for up to 2 months. Defrost, then reheat in the oven at 180°C/350°F/Gas 4 for about 20 minutes, or until heated through.

SALMON AND BUTTERNUT SQUASH BALLS

These are just perfect for little fingers! The butternut squash makes the balls lovely and soft and the couscous adds a slight crunch in texture when baked in the oven.

2 tsp olive oil

100g/3½oz butternut squash, peeled and grated

100g/3½oz cooked and cooled couscous

1 small onion, diced

300g/11oz skinless salmon fillet, diced

50g/2oz parmesan cheese, grated

1 tbsp sweet chilli sauce

3 tbsp plain flour

Preheat the oven to 200°C/400°F/Gas 6 and line a baking sheet with baking parchment.

Heat the oil in a small frying pan over a medium heat, add the squash and fry for 3–5 minutes until just softened, then remove from the heat and leave to cool.

Put the squash and the remaining ingredients (except the flour) in a food processor and blitz until finely chopped. Transfer the mixture to a bowl and shape it into 20 balls.

Coat the balls lightly with flour, place on the lined baking sheet and bake for 15 minutes until lightly golden and cooked through.

The cooked balls can be frozen (once cooled) for up to 8 weeks. Defrost, then reheat in the oven at 180°C/350°F/Gas 4 for about 10 minutes, or until heated through.

SALMON AND COD BURGERS

It's so important to include fish in your child's diet and we know that the healthy fats in oily fish such as salmon encourage growth and development. But it doesn't have to be boring: try these tasty salmon and cod burgers with my homemade tartare sauce.

2 tbsp sunflower oil
6 mini brioche buns
6 lettuce leaves
6 tomato slices

BURGERS
125g/4½oz skinless salmon fillet, diced
125g/4½oz skinless cod fillet, diced
6 spring onions, chopped
50g/2oz parmesan cheese, grated
1 tbsp tomato ketchup
1 tbsp mayonnaise
30g/1¼oz panko or dried breadcrumbs

TARTAR SAUCE
100g/3½oz mayonnaise
30g/1¼oz gherkins, finely chopped
2 spring onions, finely chopped
1 tsp chopped fresh flat-leaf parsley leaves
squeeze of lemon juice

To make the burgers, put all of the ingredients in a food processor and blitz until finely chopped. Transfer the mixture to a bowl and shape it into 6 burgers.

Heat the sunflower oil in a large frying pan over a medium heat, add the burgers and fry for 3–4 minutes on each side (fry in batches if necessary) until lightly golden and cooked through.

Combine all the ingredients for the tartar sauce in a small bowl.

Slice the buns in half. Arrange some lettuce on top of one half of each bun, then add the burgers, top with tomato slices, some tartar sauce, then finally the other half of each bun.

The cooked burgers can be frozen (once cooled) for up to 2 months. Defrost, then reheat in the oven at 180°C/350°F/ Gas 4 for about 12 minutes, or until heated through.

TIP

When using fresh herbs such as parsley, hold them in small bunches and snip with kitchen scissors. It's a lot faster and the herbs will not be bruised as they often are when they are chopped.

TERIYAKI CHICKEN BALLS

This is not one to be missed. It's so quick and easy to prepare! Simply mix grated carrot, apple and fresh ginger with chicken, onion and breadcrumbs, bake in the oven, then toss them in a delicious Japanese glaze. Serve as they are for a snack, or with rice and vegetables for a main meal.

---

1 onion, chopped
½ large apple, peeled and grated
1 large carrot, grated
1 tsp grated fresh root ginger
500g/1lb 2oz chicken thigh fillets, diced
40g/1½oz panko or dried breadcrumbs
salt and pepper

GLAZE
5 tbsp mirin
2 tbsp soy sauce
1 tbsp caster sugar
1 tsp rice wine vinegar
squeeze of lemon juice

Preheat the oven to 200°C/400°F/Gas 6 and line a baking sheet with baking parchment.

Put the onion, apple, carrot and ginger in a food processor with the chicken and breadcrumbs and blitz until finely chopped.

Transfer the mixture to a bowl, season with a little salt and pepper and shape into 30 balls. Place the balls on the lined baking sheet and bake in the oven for 15 minutes until cooked through.

Meanwhile, put all the glaze ingredients in a frying pan and simmer for 2 minutes until reduced slightly. Add the chicken balls to the pan and heat through for about 2 minutes until the glaze has coated the balls.

The cooked chicken balls can be frozen (once cooled) for up to 2 months. Defrost, then reheat in the oven at 180°C/350°F/Gas 4 for about 12 minutes, or until heated through.

MINI CAULIFLOWER PIZZAS

Who would imagine that grated cauliflower could make a tasty base for a pizza? Add your favourite pizza toppings to keep the takeaway at bay.

BASE
300g/11oz cauliflower
1 egg, beaten
100g/3½oz mature cheddar
   cheese, grated

TOMATO SAUCE
1 tbsp sunflower oil
½ red onion, finely chopped
1 garlic clove, crushed
200g/7oz tinned chopped
   tomatoes
2 tbsp chopped fresh basil

TOPPINGS
50g/2oz diced cooked chicken
4 tbsp tinned sweetcorn
25g/1oz parmesan cheese,
   grated

Preheat the oven to 180°C/350°F/Gas 4 and line a baking sheet with baking parchment.

Coarsely grate the cauliflower into a microwave-safe bowl. Put the bowl into the microwave and cook on high for 5 minutes, stirring the cauliflower halfway through. Leave to cool for 10 minutes, then transfer the cauliflower to a clean tea towel or piece of muslin, enclose it tightly and squeeze out all of the liquid until the cauliflower is dry. Return the cauliflower to the bowl and mix in the beaten egg and grated cheese.

Shape the cauliflower mixture into 4 round pizza bases on the baking sheet. Bake for 20 minutes until lightly golden and firm.

Meanwhile, make the tomato sauce. Heat the oil in a small saucepan, add the onion and fry for 3–5 minutes until softened but not browned. Add the garlic and fry for 30 seconds, then add the tomatoes and simmer for 10 minutes until thick and reduced. Remove from the heat and add the basil. Spread the sauce over the bases and top with the chicken, sweetcorn and Parmesan. Put the pizzas back in the oven for 10–15 minutes until lightly golden on top.

VARIATION
Play around with the toppings. You could try pepperoni, diced sweet pepper, cherry tomatoes, mushrooms, basil and mozzarella.

MEATBALLS WITH ORZO

It's important to keep mealtimes interesting for children and orzo is a great alternative to pasta. This dish is pure comfort in a bowl and full of goodness – it's the ultimate failsafe family pleaser.

50g/2oz white bread, crusts removed

4 tbsp milk

300g/11oz minced beef

1 onion, finely chopped

½ apple, peeled and grated

1 tsp chopped fresh thyme leaves

a few drops of Worcestershire sauce

250g/9oz orzo pasta

2 tbsp sunflower oil

TOMATO SAUCE

1 tbsp sunflower oil

1 onion, finely chopped

2 garlic cloves, crushed

2 x 400g/14oz tins chopped tomatoes

1 tbsp sun-dried tomato paste

pinch of sugar

2 tbsp chopped fresh basil leaves

10g/¼oz parmesan cheese, grated

To make the meatballs, put the bread and milk in a bowl and leave to soak for 5 minutes, then mash with a fork. Put the soaked bread in a food processor with the remaining meatball ingredients (except the pasta and oil) and blitz until finely chopped. Transfer the mixture to a bowl and shape it into 24 balls.

To make the tomato sauce, heat the oil in a saucepan over a medium heat, add the onion and fry for 5 minutes until softened, then add the garlic and fry for 30 seconds. Add the chopped tomatoes, tomato paste and sugar, bring to the boil, then reduce the heat, cover and simmer for 10 minutes. Remove from the heat and add the basil and parmesan.

Heat the sunflower oil in a large frying pan over a high heat, add the meatballs and fry for 4–5 minutes until golden brown. Add them to the tomato sauce and simmer for 5 minutes.

Cook the orzo in a pan of boiling water according to the packet instructions, drain and serve with the meatballs and sauce.

The meatballs and sauce can be frozen (once cooled) for up to 2 months. Defrost, then reheat in a saucepan or in the microwave until piping hot.

CRISPY BAKED COD WITH SWEET POTATO CHIPS

Fish and chips can still very much be on the menu if you're trying to put more healthy food on the family table – simply make a few tweaks so it's less 'naughty' and more nutritious.

4 tbsp plain flour

1 egg, beaten

40g/1½oz cornflakes, crushed

2 skinless cod fillets (about 150g/5oz)

salt and pepper

SWEET POTATO CHIPS

3 sweet potatoes, cut into wedges

2 tbsp sunflower oil

Preheat the oven to 200°C/400°F/Gas 6 and line 2 baking sheets with baking parchment.

Put the flour in a bowl, the beaten egg in another bowl and the crushed cornflakes in a third bowl.

Season the cod with a little salt and pepper and coat each fillet in the flour, then the egg, then the crushed cornflakes. Arrange the coated fillets on one of the lined baking sheets.

Toss the sweet potato wedges with the oil, season lightly with salt and pepper and spread them out on the second lined baking sheet. Put the sweet potato chips in the oven and bake for 30 minutes, turning the chips halfway through the cooking time. When you turn the chips, add the fish to the oven and bake for 15 minutes until golden and cooked through.

Remove the chips and baked cod from the oven and serve straight away, with the cod wrapped in paper cones if you wish.

GRANOLA WITH YOGHURT AND BERRIES

Once you've made this you will ditch shop-bought granola. It's so easy to make. Packed with oats, dried fruits, nuts and seeds, it's full of essential vitamins, healthy fats and fibre to set the whole family up for the day ahead.

150g/5oz porridge oats

40g/1½oz pecan nuts, finely chopped

30g/1¼oz desiccated coconut

50g/2oz soft light brown sugar

25g/1oz sunflower seeds

25g/1oz pumpkin seeds

1 tbsp chia seeds

½ tsp mixed spice

pinch of salt

50g/2oz maple syrup

25ml/1fl oz sunflower oil

50g/2oz sultanas

50g/2oz dried cranberries, chopped

TO SERVE

plain yoghurt

maple syrup

fresh mixed berries

Preheat the oven to 150°C/300°F/Gas 2 and line a large baking tray with baking parchment.

Put the oats, pecan nuts, coconut, sugar, seeds, mixed spice and salt in a large bowl and toss together.

Whisk the maple syrup and oil together, pour it over the dry ingredients and mix to coat. Tip onto the lined baking tray and spread it out evenly.

Bake the granola in the oven for 30–35 minutes, stirring it every 10 minutes until golden and toasted.

Remove from the oven, leave to cool, the add the sultanas and cranberries. Store in an airtight container for up to 2 weeks.

To serve, you can layer the granola in glasses with yoghurt drizzled with maple syrup and berries.

CHAPTER 5

LUNCHBOX & PLAYDATE SNACKS

GIANT COUSCOUS SALAD WITH RAINBOW VEGGIES AND CHICKEN

Kids often eat with their eyes, so here's a great way to make salad that little bit more appealing. It squeezes in lots of different veggies too.

125g/4½oz giant couscous
1 carrot, diced
1 red pepper, deseeded and finely diced
4 spring onions, sliced
100g/3½oz cooked and shelled edamame
180g/6oz cooked chicken, diced
198g/7oz tin sweetcorn, drained
salt and pepper

DRESSING
3 tbsp olive oil
1 tbsp rice wine vinegar
1 tsp good-quality balsamic vinegar
2 tsp maple syrup

Cook the giant couscous according to the packet instructions.

Put the couscous in a large bowl with the remaining ingredients, mix to combine and season well with salt and pepper.

Whisk together the dressing ingredients in a bowl, pour over the salad, toss and serve.

VARIATION
Vegetarian Giant Couscous Salad
Cook 200g/7oz giant couscous. Swap the chicken, soya beans and spring onions for 2 tbsp chopped chives, 30g/1¼oz chopped dried cranberries and 50g/2oz chopped pecans. Mix with the cooked couscous in a bowl. Fry a sliced red onion in 1 tbsp olive oil until soft, add 3 tbsp more oil, 2 tbsp each of soy sauce, mirin and rice wine vinegar. Swirl in the pan then pour over the couscous and serve.

TURKEY AND CUCUMBER ROLL-UP

Large sandwiches and wraps can be a little overwhelming for mini eaters, so why not liven up your child's lunch break with my fun bite-sized roll ups. They are super simple and sure to be a hit. Turkey is also a fantastic source of protein and zinc, which is important for a healthy immune system, making this an ideal lunchbox filler.

1 tortilla
1 tbsp mayonnaise
1 tsp sweet chilli sauce
2 slices of cooked turkey
2 thin strips of cucumber

Warm the tortilla in the microwave for 20 seconds then place it on a chopping board.

Spread the mayonnaise and chilli sauce over the wrap, top with the turkey and put 2 strips of cucumber on one side of the turkey slices.

Roll up the wrap so the cucumber is in the middle and slice into bite-sized pieces.

VARIATION
Chicken and Cucumber Roll-Up
Swap the chilli sauce for plum sauce and the cooked turkey for 50g/2oz shredded cooked chicken, adding a finely sliced spring onion if you like.

PASTRAMI ROLL-UP

Here's a 3-minute roll-up for when you want something tasty and you are in a hurry.

1 tortilla
2 tsp fresh green pesto
2 slices of pastrami
1 slice edam cheese, chopped
1 tomato, chopped

Put the tortilla on a chopping board.

Spread the pesto over the wrap. Lay the pastrami on top, scatter with chopped cheese and tomato, roll up tightly and slice into 4 bite-sized pieces.

VARIATION
Tomato, Mozzarella and Pesto Roll-Up
Mix 1 tbsp of mayonnaise into the pesto before spreading it over the wrap. Swap the pastrami and edam for 50g/2oz sliced mozzarella and chop the tomato instead of slicing it. Sprinkle over a few basil leaves and roll it up.

TASTY CHICKEN AND POTATO SALAD

A classic potato salad traditionally comes dressed with mayonnaise but my dairy-free version is leaner, lighter and just as tasty. The chicken and potato soak up the delicious flavours of the dressing and it's suitable for children aged 8 months up so it really is a recipe to feed the whole family – from toddler to teen.

250g/9oz baby new potatoes, halved
3 spring onions, thinly sliced
50g/2oz deseeded cucumber, finely diced
5 cherry tomatoes, quartered
25g/1oz deseeded red pepper, diced
75g/3oz cooked chicken, finely diced

DRESSING
1½ tbsp white wine vinegar
4 tbsp olive oil
1 tsp soy sauce
1 tsp maple syrup

Cook the baby new potatoes in a pan of boiling water for 12–15 minutes, or until tender, then drain and leave to cool.

When cold, mix the cooked potatoes, spring onions, cucumber, tomatoes, red pepper and chicken together in a bowl.

Whisk the dressing ingredients together in a small jug or bowl and pour over the salad. Toss together and serve.

CHICKEN PASTA SALAD WITH BROCCOLI

You can make this tasty salad in 10 minutes. It is easy to prepare the night before you need it. All you have to do is toss in the dressing in the morning and pop it in your child's lunchbox or, even better, put the salad dressing in a small pot and let your child add the dressing just before eating.

110g/4oz fusilli pasta
100g/3½oz broccoli florets
100g/3½oz cooked chicken
    breast, chopped
100g/3½oz tinned sweetcorn
10 cherry tomatoes
4 spring onions, thinly sliced
salt and pepper

DRESSING
3 tbsp light olive oil
1 tbsp rice wine vinegar
1½ tsp honey
½ tsp Dijon mustard

Cook the pasta in a pan of boiling salted water according to the packet instructions, then drain.

While the pasta is cooking, steam the broccoli florets for about 4 minutes.

Meanwhile, whisk together the dressing ingredients.

Put the chopped chicken, sweetcorn, tomatoes and spring onions in a bowl together with the drained pasta and broccoli and toss with the dressing.

FRITTATA MUFFINS

A simple way to make individual frittatas is to bake them in a muffin tin. Try substituting the ham for diced chicken or crumbled bacon, or for a vegetarian version leave out the ham and add some grilled red pepper, some peas or diced courgette and maybe some feta cheese.

sunflower oil, for greasing
3 large eggs
2 tbsp milk
40g/1½oz mature cheddar cheese, grated
1 tomato, deseeded and finely chopped
3 spring onions, finely chopped
100g/3½oz cooked cold potatoes, diced (use leftover cooked potatoes if you have any to hand)
2 tbsp chopped fresh basil leaves
2 thick slices of ham, diced
salt and pepper

Preheat the oven to 180°C/350°F/Gas 4 and grease a 6-hole muffin tin with sunflower oil (or 6 holes of a 12-hole tin).

Beat the eggs and milk together in a bowl. Stir in the remaining ingredients and season lightly with salt and pepper. Spoon the mixture evenly between the greased muffin holes and bake in the oven for 15–20 minutes until set and risen.

Remove from the oven and leave to cool for a few minutes in the tin before removing with a palette knife. Eat hot or cold. They will keep in the fridge for up to 2 days.

CARROT, CHEESE AND TOMATO MUFFINS

Kids won't often turn down a muffin so they are a great way to experiment with different foods and flavours. This adventurous little number features carrot, sun-dried tomato and spring onion to liven up little ones' lunchtimes.

175g/6oz self-raising flour
1 tsp baking powder
2 eggs, beaten
2 tbsp maple syrup
6 tbsp milk
50g/2oz parmesan cheese, grated
3 spring onions, chopped
75g/3oz carrot, grated
pinch of salt
8 sun-dried tomatoes in oil, chopped

Preheat the oven to 180°C/350°F/Gas 4 and line a 12-hole muffin tin with 10 paper cases.

Mix the flour and baking powder in a large bowl then add all of the remaining ingredients and stir until just combined (avoid over-mixing it).

Spoon the mixture into the muffin cases and bake in the oven for 18–20 minutes until well risen and lightly golden.

Remove from the oven, remove the muffins from the tin (still in their cases) and leave to cool on a wire rack.

The muffins can be frozen (once cooled) for up to 2 months. Defrost then reheat in the oven at 180°C/350°F/Gas 4 for 8–10 minutes until heated through.

AFTER-SCHOOL VEGGIE PLATTER

Children love to be offered choice when it comes to mealtimes and this platter is a real feast for the eyes. The more interesting the platter looks, the more they will be drawn to it and the more open they will be to trying new foods. Children also often like to eat with their fingers, so this is perfect for tiny hands! More manageable mouthfuls are less overwhelming for a small child, too.

60g/2¼oz broccoli florets
70g/2¾oz cooked and shelled edamame
2 carrots, cut into batons
6 cherry tomatoes, halved
6 slices of pastrami
3 slices of gruyere cheese

DIP
4 tbsp sour cream
½ garlic clove, crushed
1 tbsp chopped chives

Cook the broccoli in a pan of boiling water for 3–4 minutes, drain and refresh under cold running water. Drain well.

Arrange the broccoli, edamame, carrots and cherry tomatoes on a plate or platter.

Put half a slice of pastrami on a chopping board. Put half a slice of cheese on top. Roll up to make a cylinder, slice in half and push a cocktail stick through to hold the roll together. Repeat until you have 12 pastrami and cheese sticks.

Mix the dip ingredients in a bowl. Put the dip in the middle of the the plate or platter and arrange the pastrami and cheese sticks next to the vegetables.

VEGGIE LUNCHBOX TRAYBAKE

Here's a stealthy, simple and super tasty way to pack in those veggies. It's a good recipe for children to get involved in: after they've helped make it they can take some extra portions in their lunchbox to share with their friends.

225g/8oz self-raising flour

1 tsp baking powder

large pinch of salt

65g/2½oz butter, chilled and diced

2 large eggs, beaten

80ml/3fl oz whole milk

50g/2oz cheddar cheese, grated

50g/2oz parmesan cheese, grated

175g/6oz courgette, grated

175g/6oz carrot, grated

6 spring onions, finely chopped

2 tsp dried oregano

2 tomatoes, finely chopped

Preheat the oven to 180°C/350°F/Gas 4 and line a 23cm/9in square baking tin with baking parchment.

Put the flour, baking powder, salt and butter in a bowl. Rub the butter into the flour with your fingertips until well incorporated, then add the eggs, milk and grated cheeses (you could blitz the flour and butter in a food processor before adding the wet ingredients if you prefer, just pulsing briefly to incorporate the wet ingredients with the butter and flour). Add the vegetables and oregano, mix well, spoon into the tin and level out the top.

Bake in the oven for 30–35 minutes until lightly golden and well risen, then remove and leave to cool on a wire rack.

Turn out the cooled traybake from the baking tin and cut into 16 squares. The traybake will keep for up to 2 days in the fridge.

'SUSHI' SANDWICHES

There's no reason why children can't enjoy sushi! My sushi-style wraps are an ingenious way to get kids trying new ingredients. Replacing sushi rice with bread makes for a quick and inexpensive lunchbox pleaser. Chopsticks at the ready.

4 slices of white bread, crusts removed

a little softened butter

2 slices of brown bread, crusts removed

CHICKEN AND SWEETCORN

40g/1½oz cooked chicken, finely diced

1 tbsp mayonnaise

1 tbsp tinned sweetcorn

½ large carrot, grated

BEEF, TOMATO AND LETTUCE

2 tbsp mayonnaise

40g/1½oz cooked beef, thinly sliced

2 lettuce leaves

1 tomato, deseeded and thinly sliced

PRAWN

100g/3½oz cooked peeled prawns, drained and chopped

2 tbsp mayonnaise

4 cucumber batons

1 tomato, deseeded and thinly sliced

Put the white bread slices on a chopping board, cover with clingfilm and roll them out with a rolling pin to a thickness of 3mm/⅛in. Remove the clingfilm and spread the flattened slices with butter.

For the chicken and sweetcorn filling, mix the chicken, mayonnaise and sweetcorn together in a bowl. Spoon along the sides of 2 buttered slices of bread. Top with the grated carrot, roll each slice up tightly, then cut each roll into 3 pieces.

For the beef, tomato and lettuce filling, spread the mayonnaise over the remaining 2 slices of flattened white bread. Put the beef on one edge of the mayo-covered bread slices, top with lettuce and tomato, roll up and trim the edges, the cut each roll into 3 pieces.

For the prawn filling, put the brown bread slices on a chopping board, cover with clingfilm and roll them out with a rolling pin to a thickness of 3mm/⅛in. Mix the prawns and mayonnaise together in a bowl. Spoon onto one edge of each bread slice. Top with cucumber and tomato, roll up tightly and trim the edges. Slice each roll into 3 pieces.

CHICKEN, SWEETCORN AND CARROT BALLS

Ever had a last-minute playdate to prep for? My chicken, sweetcorn and carrot balls will satisfy hungry tums in no time at all. Quick, easy and nutritious, they prove the perfect after-school snack.

2 skinless chicken breasts (about 300g/11oz), diced
½ red onion, chopped
2 tbsp tinned sweetcorn
75g/3oz carrot, grated
1 tbsp chopped fresh thyme leaves
40g/1½oz panko or dried breadcrumbs
¾ chicken stock cube, crushed
1 tbsp sweet chilli sauce
1 tbsp plain flour
2 tbsp sunflower oil
salt and pepper

Put the chicken breasts in a food processor and blitz until roughly chopped. Add the remaining ingredients (except the flour and oil), season lightly with salt and pepper and blitz together until everything is finely chopped.

Transfer the mixture to a bowl and shape it into 25 balls. Coat the balls in flour.

Heat the oil in a frying pan over a medium heat and fry the balls in batches for 8–10 minutes until golden and cooked through.

The cooked balls can be frozen (once cooled) for up to 2 months. Defrost, then reheat in the oven at 180°C/350°F/Gas 4 for about 20 minutes, or until heated through.

ENERGY BALLS WITH PEANUT BUTTER, DATES AND PUMPKIN SEEDS

Snacking on healthy food when you're on the go is sometimes easier said than done. I always make sure I have a batch of these energy balls on hand for those busy days. Packed with oats, peanut butter and pumpkin seeds and naturally sweetened with dates, they are ideal finger food and will help give your child (along with the rest of the family) a mid-morning or afternoon energy boost. They are also delicious alongside a cup of coffee!

150g/5oz pitted dates, chopped
2 tbsp smooth peanut butter
2 tbsp sunflower oil
1 tbsp maple syrup
30g/1¼oz desiccated coconut
85g/3oz porridge oats
2 tbsp flaxseeds
30g/1¼oz dried cranberries, chopped
15g/½oz Rice Krispies
2 tbsp pumpkin seeds
pinch of salt

Put the chopped dates in a saucepan over a medium heat with 85ml/3¼fl oz boiling water. Cover and cook for 3–4 minutes, depending on how hard the dates are, then blend until smooth with an electric stick blender. Add the peanut butter, oil and maple syrup to the pan and stir gently until melted. Remove from the heat.

Add the remaining ingredients and stir until combined. Shape the mixture into 18–20 balls and chill on a plate in the fridge for at least 30 minutes to firm up before eating.

The balls will keep for up to 5 days in an airtight container in the fridge.

PITTA POCKETS

In need of some lunchbox or after-school snack inspiration? Make sure your kids try these filled pitta pockets.

2 wholemeal pitta breads
2 white pitta breads

TUNA
120g/4½oz tin tuna in oil,
   drained
3 tbsp mayonnaise
1 tsp sweet chilli sauce
1 tbsp chopped chives
1 egg, hard-boiled and
   thinly sliced
2 cherry tomatoes, thinly sliced

CORONATION CHICKEN
3 tbsp mayonnaise
1 tsp apricot jam
½ tsp mild curry powder
½ tsp tomato puree
squeeze of lemon juice
100g/3½oz cooked chicken
   breast, diced
a few lettuce leaves, shredded
salt and pepper

Lightly toast the pitta breads in the toaster, then slice each pitta in half to make 8 pitta pockets (don't toast them if they're going in a lunchbox).

To make the tuna filling, mix the tuna, mayonnaise, sweet chilli sauce and chives in a bowl. Fill 4 of the pitta pockets with the filling, adding the sliced egg and tomatoes, too.

To make the coronation chicken filling, mix the mayonnaise, jam, curry powder, tomato puree and lemon juice in a bowl. Add the chicken and season lightly with salt and pepper. Fill the remaining 4 pitta pockets with the chicken filling and shredded lettuce.

Serve straight away.

TIP

Adding a little salt or vinegar to the pan when cooking boiled eggs will prevent the egg from leaking out of its shell if it cracks in the water.

VEGETABLE TRAIN

2 yellow peppers
1 red pepper
1 cucumber
2 white or brown pitta breads
50g/2oz baby corn
2 carrots

GUACAMOLE
2 ripe avocados, stoned, peeled
    and diced
1 ripe tomato, roughly chopped
1 large garlic clove, crushed
2 tbsp chopped fresh flat-leaf
    parsley leaves
juice of ½ lemon
pinch of red chilli flakes
    (optional)
salt and pepper

THOUSAND ISLAND DIP
4 tbsp Greek yoghurt
4 tbsp mayonnaise
1 heaped tsp tomato ketchup
1 tsp lemon juice
a couple of drops of
    Worcestershire sauce

HUMMUS
400g/14oz tin chickpeas,
    drained
1 garlic clove, crushed
6 tbsp olive oil
2 tbsp Greek yoghurt
juice of ½ small lemon

Interestingly, children who don't like cooked veggies will often eat them raw. This colourful train laden with crudités will delight even the most hardened veggie hater. And then there is the extra thrill of using the crudités to scoop some tasty dips.

Cut out a rectangle shape on one side of all of the peppers to make the train carriages. Discard the seeds. Push 4 cocktail sticks into the bottom of each piece of pepper to attach the wheels. Slice 3mm/⅛in-thick track rounds from the cucumber and carrot and attach 4 wheels to the peppers. Slice the leftover pepper into strips, cut the leftover carrots into batons and slice the remaining cucumber into batons.

Toast the pitta breads and slice them into 2.5cm/1in strips. Arrange the vegetables and pitta bread in the train carriages and assemble on a board or tray.

To make the guacamole, put all of the ingredients in a bowl, season lightly with salt and pepper and blitz with an electric stick blender until smooth.

To make the Thousand Island dip, simply combine all the ingredients in a bowl.

To make the hummus, put all the ingredients in a food processor, blitz until smooth and season to taste.

Serve the dips alongside the train.

TUNA POKE BOWL

170g/6oz quinoa
75g/3oz edamame
200g/7oz fresh tuna, diced
4 spring onions, sliced
1 ripe avocado, stoned, peeled
  and diced
3 tbsp sprouting beans
2 tbsp sesame seeds, toasted

MARINADE
2 tsp rice wine vinegar
2 tsp sesame oil
2 tbsp soy sauce
pinch of red chilli flakes
  (optional)
squeeze of lemon juice

DRESSING
2 tbsp soy sauce
1 tbsp rice wine vinegar
1 tbsp sesame oil
3 tbsp olive oil
pinch of sugar

CRISPY SHALLOTS
sunflower oil, for frying
4 banana shallots, sliced
salt

Originating from Hawaii, poke bowls are now very popular and are a bit like deconstructed sushi – I have used quinoa here but poke bowls are often made with rice. 'Poke' means 'to cut' and this dish uses diced good-quality fresh tuna: it's a super healthy salad for a tasty light lunch. If you're putting it in a lunchbox, keep it cool with ice packs.

Cook the quinoa in a pan of boiling water according to the packet instructions, drain and leave to cool.

Cook the edamame in boiling water for 5 minutes, drain and refresh under cold running water.

Mix all of the marinade ingredients together in a bowl. Add the tuna and spring onions. Stir, cover and leave to marinate in the fridge for 30 minutes.

Mix all of the dressing ingredients together in a jug.

Spoon the cooked quinoa into 4 small bowls. Put the marinated tuna on top. Add the diced avocado, sprouting beans and edamame. Pour over the dressing and sprinkle with the toasted sesame seeds.

To make the crispy shallots, pour sunflower oil into a small saucepan to a depth of 2cm /¾in. Place over a medium-high heat until very hot. Add half the sliced shallots and fry them for 1–2 minutes until golden. Remove from the pan with a slotted spoon and transfer to kitchen paper to drain, cool and crisp up. Sprinkle with a little salt. Repeat with the remaining shallots and scatter on top of the tuna just before serving.

CRANBERRY AND SULTANA FLAPJACKS

Keeping kids energised throughout the day while they're at school is so important. The dried fruit in these flapjacks contains fibre and iron, the nuts provide those all-important omega 3s and the oats help release energy slowly throughout the afternoon, keeping little learners fuelled for longer. Flapjacks are also fun for kids to make themselves, then pop in their lunchbox with some extra to share with friends.

100g/3½oz unsalted butter
100g/3½oz golden caster sugar
80g/3oz golden syrup
125g/4½oz porridge oats
30g/1¼oz pecan nuts, finely chopped
50g/2oz sultanas
20g/¾oz desiccated coconut
50g/2oz dried cranberries
10g/¼oz chia seeds

Preheat the oven to 160°C/325°F/Gas 3 and line a 20cm/8in square baking tin with baking parchment.

Melt the butter with the caster sugar and syrup in a saucepan over a low heat until runny.

Remove from the heat, add the oats, chopped pecan nuts, sultanas, desiccated coconut, cranberries and chia seeds and mix together.

Spoon the mixture into the lined tin, level the top, and bake for 20 minutes until golden brown and just set in the middle. Remove and leave to cool in the tin for 10 minutes before turning it out onto a wire rack and removing the parchment. Leave to cool fully, then slice into 8 bars or 16 squares.

The flapjacks will keep in an airtight container for up to 1 week.

CARROT CAKE BALLS

Carrot cake is a favourite of mine so I have turned this much-loved teatime treat into healthy bite-sized snack. Adding a little mixed spice awakens those taste buds and encourages kids to try new flavour combinations.

100g/3½oz pitted dates, chopped
100g/3½oz carrots
40g/1½oz pecan nuts
50g/2oz sultanas
1 tbsp sunflower oil
50g/2oz porridge oats
1 tsp mixed spice
pinch of salt
40g/1½oz desiccated coconut

Put the chopped dates in a saucepan over a medium heat with 50ml/2fl oz boiling water. Cover and cook for 2 minutes.

Put the carrots in a food processor and blitz until roughly chopped. Add the dates, along with their soaking water, and all the remaining ingredients (leaving half the desiccated coconut aside for rolling) and blitz until the mixture comes together.

Transfer the mixture to a bowl and shape into 16 balls. Roll the balls in the remaining desiccated coconut and chill on a plate in the fridge for at least 30 minutes to firm up before eating.

The carrot cake balls will keep in an airtight container in the fridge for up to 5 days.

CHAPTER 6

DESSERTS
&
SWEETS

PLUM AND BLUEBERRY CRUMBLE

Crumble is such a great dessert option: it's so easy to prepare and never disappoints. Swap the plums and blueberries for your family's favourite fruit or choose what's in season for a versatile year-round pud.

1 tbsp ground almonds
30g/1¼oz butter
1kg/2¼lb ripe red plums, halved and stoned
50g/2oz light muscovado sugar
150g/5oz blueberries

CRUMBLE TOPPING
150g/5oz plain flour
175g/6oz light muscovado sugar
150g/5oz ground almonds
150g/5oz unsalted butter, chilled and diced
generous pinch of salt
1 tbsp demerara sugar

Preheat the oven to 180°C/350°F/Gas 4. Sprinkle the almonds over the base of a shallow baking dish, about 2 litre/3½ pint capacity.

Melt the butter in a large saucepan over a medium heat, add the plums and sprinkle with the muscovado sugar. Cook for 5 minutes (or less if the plums are very ripe) until soft. Spoon the plums and cooking liquid into the dish and scatter over the blueberries.

To make the crumble topping, put the flour, muscovado sugar, ground almonds, butter and salt in a food processor and blitz until the fine crumbs are just starting to cling together (avoid over-processing the mixture). Alternatively, rub the butter into the flour, ground almonds, sugar and salt in a bowl with your fingertips.

Scatter the crumble topping over the fruit and sprinkle the crumble with the demerara sugar. Bake in the oven for 30–35 minutes until the crumble is lightly golden and bubbling at the edges.

The cooked crumble can be frozen (once cooled) for up to 2 months. Defrost, then reheat in the oven at 180°C/350°F/Gas 4 for about 20 minutes, or until heated through.

FRENCH TOAST WITH BERRY COMPOTE

My French toast triangles are the most heavenly breakfast treat. Top with a spoonful of berry compote or a dollop of yoghurt and a drizzle of maple syrup.

2 eggs, beaten
2 tbsp milk
2 medium slices of country-style
   crusty bread
knob of butter
2 tsp icing sugar
3 tbsp natural yoghurt
maple syrup, to taste

BERRY COMPOTE
knob of butter
150g/5oz blueberries and
   blackberries
1 tbsp caster sugar
75g/3oz raspberries

Beat the eggs and milk together in a wide, shallow bowl. Add the bread slices and soak them in the egg mixture for 1 minute.

Melt the butter in a frying pan over a medium heat, add the soaked slices of bread and fry for 1–2 minutes on each side until golden, then sprinkle each slice with a teaspoon of icing sugar. Remove from the heat, cut each slice into triangles and arrange them on 2 plates.

To make the compote, melt the butter in a saucepan over a medium heat. Add the blueberries, blackberries and sugar and stir over the heat for 1 minute until the sugar has dissolved. Remove from the heat and add the raspberries.

Spoon the compote over the French toast triangles, add a dollop of yoghurt and drizzle with maple syrup.

RICE KRISPIE, OAT AND APRICOT BARS

These fruity oat bars are super soft, moist and delicious. They require no baking, so you can make them in just 10 minutes with your little one then pop them in the fridge to set. They won't last long ...

150g/5oz porridge oats
50g/2oz Rice Krispies
50g/2oz dried apricots, chopped
50g/2oz chopped pecan nuts
 (optional)
100g/3½oz unsalted butter
85g/3¼oz golden syrup
75g/3oz white chocolate, broken
 into pieces
pinch of salt

Line a shallow 28 x 18cm/11 x 7in tin with baking parchment.

Combine the oats, Rice Krispies, chopped apricots and pecan nuts (if using) in a bowl.

Put the butter, golden syrup, white chocolate and salt in a large saucepan over a low heat and heat through, stirring occasionally, until melted and combined.

Stir the oat and Rice Krispie mixture into the melted chocolate mixture until well coated.

Press the mixture into the lined tin, using a potato masher to level the surface, and put in the fridge for about 2 hours to set. Cut into 10 bars.

TIP

When using golden syrup, warm
your spoon in hot water before
measuring out the syrup and it will
slide off easily.

OAT, RAISIN AND SUNFLOWER SEED COOKIES

Interestingly, allergy to eggs is the commonest allergy in children. These cookies are egg-free and super delicious. And you only need a handful of storecupboard ingredients. The oats and sunflower seeds help to release energy slowly throughout the day while the raisins add a welcome hit of fruity sweetness.

85g/3¼oz softened unsalted butter
75g/3oz soft light brown sugar
1 tsp vanilla extract
75g/3oz raisins
40g/1½oz sunflower seeds
75g/3oz plain flour
75g/3oz porridge oats
½ tsp bicarbonate of soda
½ tsp fine salt

Preheat the oven to 180°C/350°F/Gas 4 and line 2 baking sheets with baking parchment.

Put the butter and sugar in a large mixing bowl and cream together using an electric hand-held whisk until light and fluffy (or use a stand mixer), then add the remaining ingredients and mix until combined to form a dough.

Divide the dough into 14 equal portions, then roll the portions into balls. Put the balls on the lined baking sheets, ensuring you leave a space of at least 5cm/2in around each ball as they will spread when they bake. Flatten them slightly with a spatula, then bake in the oven for 12–15 minutes, or until lightly golden.

Remove the cookies from the oven and leave to cool for a few minutes on the baking sheets before transferring to a wire rack to cool completely.

The cookies will keep in an airtight container for up to 3 days, or can be frozen after baking. To defrost, simply leave at room temperature.

BLUEBERRY MUFFINS

Get your own mini chefs to help you cook up these beautiful blueberry muffins. The Greek yoghurt and fresh blueberries keep the mixture moist and moreish.

250g/9oz self-raising flour
1 tsp bicarbonate of soda
100g/3½oz caster sugar
grated zest of ½ lemon
2 large eggs
150g/5oz Greek yoghurt
100g/3½oz unsalted butter,
  melted
1 tsp vanilla extract
150g/5oz blueberries
3 tbsp demerara sugar

Preheat the oven to 180°C/350°F/Gas 4 and line a 12-hole muffin tin with 12 paper cases.

Put the flour, bicarbonate of soda, caster sugar and lemon zest in a large bowl and mix. Put the eggs, yoghurt, melted butter and vanilla extract in another bowl and whisk until smooth. Add the wet ingredients to the dry ingredients and whisk with an electric hand-held whisk until well combined. Stir in the blueberries.

Divide the mixture evenly between the muffin cases and sprinkle with the demerara sugar. Bake in the oven for 20–25 minutes until well risen and lightly golden brown.

Remove from the oven and leave the muffins to cool in the tin for a few minutes before transferring to a wire rack to cool completely.

The muffins will keep in an airtight container for up to 3 days, or can be frozen for up to 2 months. Defrost at room temperature.

AMARETTI AND SUMMER FRUIT GRATIN

A lighter version of crème brûlée, my summer gratin features lots of fresh fruit topped with crème fraîche and crushed amaretti biscuits. This scrumptious pud is finished under the grill and you can serve it warm or cold.

---

2 ripe peaches

3 ripe plums, halved, stoned and cut into wedges

6 strawberries, hulled and quartered

100g/3½oz raspberries

8 seedless grapes, halved

50g/2oz amaretti biscuits

300g/11oz crème fraîche

2 tbsp soft dark brown sugar

Remove the skin from the peaches by cutting a shallow cross on the bottom of each peach, placing them in a large pan of boiling water for about 20 seconds, then removing them with a slotted spoon and placing them immediately in a bowl of ice-cold water to cool. The skin should peel off easily. Halve and stone them, then slice the flesh.

Divide the prepared fruit evenly between 6 individual ramekins. Crush the amaretti biscuits in their wrappers using a rolling pin and sprinkle the biscuits on top of the fruit. Cover with the crème fraîche, sprinkle over the brown sugar and set aside in the fridge.

Preheat the grill before serving and place each gratin under the grill for a few minutes until golden.

NO-SUGAR CHOCOLATE ORANGE ENERGY BALLS

A healthy twist on a chocolate truffle – sweet-toothed tots who think they're raiding the chocolate box will be none the wiser!

160g/5½oz pitted dates, chopped
160g/5½oz cashew nuts
100g/3½oz raisins
2 tbsp cocoa powder
½ tsp orange extract

TO COAT
cocoa powder
desiccated coconut
chocolate sprinkles

Put all of the ingredients in a food processor with 4 tablespoons of boiling water and blitz until the mixture is finely chopped and well blended.

Transfer the mixture to a bowl and shape it into 15–20 balls.

Roll the balls in cocoa powder, desiccated coconut or chocolate sprinkles, as you wish. Chill on a plate in the fridge for at least 1 hour to firm up before eating.

The balls will keep in an airtight container in the fridge for up to 1 week.

SPICED APPLE, SQUASH AND CARROT MUFFINS

It's sweet, savoury and spice all in one with these mighty muffins. The grated carrot, apple and butternut squash all keep the mixture gloriously soft, plus I can't think of a better way of upping your veggie intake for the day (and I'm pretty sure kids will agree!).

150g/5oz plain wholemeal flour
50g/2oz caster sugar
1½ tsp baking powder
½ tsp ground cinnamon
¼ tsp fine salt
¼ tsp ground ginger
½ tsp mixed spice
125g/4½oz sunflower oil
120ml/4fl oz maple syrup
2 eggs, beaten
½ tsp vanilla extract
50g/2oz peeled and grated apple
50g/2oz grated carrot
50g/2oz peeled and grated
   butternut squash
60g/2¼oz raisins

Preheat the oven to 180°C/350°F/Gas 4 and line a 12-hole muffin tin with paper cases.

Put all of the dry ingredients in a bowl and mix. Put all of the wet ingredients into another bowl and stir to combine. Mix the wet ingredients into the dry ingredients gently until combined.

Divide the mixture evenly between the muffin cases and bake in the oven for 20 minutes until well risen and just firm in the middle.

Remove from the oven, leave to cool in the tin for a few minutes then transfer to a wire rack to cool completely.

The muffins will keep for up to 2 days in an airtight container.

DAIRY-FREE BEETROOT AND CHOCOLATE CAKE

You wouldn't know this chocolate cake was dairy free. It's my favourite dairy-free cake recipe and makes a fantastic birthday bake. The beetroot complements the chocolate perfectly and keeps the sponge deliciously moist.

5 eggs
200g/7oz caster sugar
225g/8oz self-raising flour
1 tsp baking powder
25g/1oz cocoa powder
200g/7oz dairy-free margarine,
    plus extra for greasing
150g/5oz cooked beetroot, grated
75g/3oz dairy-free chocolate,
    melted and cooled

ICING
100g/3½oz diary-free margarine
200g/7oz icing sugar
1 tsp vanilla extract
10g/¼oz cocoa powder
25g/1oz dairy-free chocolate

Preheat the oven to 180°C/350°F/Gas 4, grease the bases of two 20cm/8in sandwich cake tins and line them with baking parchment.

Put the eggs, caster sugar, flour, baking powder, cocoa powder and margarine in a large mixing bowl and whisk using an electric hand-held whisk until light and fluffy (or use a stand mixer). Add the beetroot and melted chocolate and whisk again. Divide the mixture evenly between the lined tins and level the top.

Bake in the oven for 28–30 minutes until well risen and firm in the middle. Remove from the oven and leave to cool in the tins for a few minutes before transferring the sponges to a wire rack to cool completely.

While the sponges are cooling, make the icing. Put the margarine, icing sugar, vanilla extract and cocoa powder in a large bowl and whisk with an electric hand-held whisk until light and fluffy (or use a stand mixer). Spread half the icing over one cake. Sandwich together with the second cake and spread the remaining icing on top. Grate the dairy-free chocolate over the top.

The cooked sponge can be frozen for up to 2 months. Defrost at room temperature.

RASPBERRY RIPPLE MINI CHEESECAKES

Raspberry ripple ice cream immediately evokes images of an English summer on the beach or playing in a sunshine-filled garden. I've taken this popular flavour (and memory) and created these mini cheesecakes as a celebration of the Great British Summertime (sometimes described as nine months of winter followed by three months of bad weather!).

BISCUIT BASE
120g/4½oz digestive biscuits
60g/2¼oz unsalted butter, melted

RASPBERRY COULIS
150g/5oz raspberries
15g/½oz icing sugar

FILLING
2 sheets leaf gelatine
250g/9oz full-fat cream cheese
100g/3½oz caster sugar
1 tsp vanilla extract
200ml/7fl oz double cream

TO DECORATE
raspberries
mint leaves

Place six 7–8cm/2¾–3in metal rings on a baking sheet lined with baking parchment.

To make the biscuit base, put the biscuits in a plastic bag and crush them with a rolling pin to form fine crumbs. Tip the crumbs into a bowl, stir in the melted butter and mix well. Press the biscuit and butter mixture into the bases of the metal rings and chill in the fridge.

Put the raspberries and icing sugar in a plastic container and blend until smooth with an electric stick blender. Pour into a fine sieve placed over a bowl and press the mixture through in order to remove the seeds.

Put the gelatine sheets in a bowl of cold water and leave for 5 minutes until soft, then put into a saucepan with 2 teaspoons of water. Gently heat until runny (do not boil) then remove from the heat and let it cool for a minute.

Beat the cream cheese, caster sugar and vanilla together in a bowl. Lightly whip the double cream in a separate bowl to soft peaks. Fold the cream cheese mixture and whipped cream together, then add the gelatine, stirring until incorporated and smooth.

Spoon one third of the cream mixture on top of the chilled biscuit bases. Drizzle a little coulis on top and swirl using a skewer to ripple. Spoon another third of the cream mixture on top, then another drizzle of raspberry coulis and swirl again. Reserve a little of the coulis for decorating the top. Put the remaining cheesecake mixture on top and smooth the surface. Place in the fridge for 3 hours to set.

Run a knife around the edges of the cheesecakes to loosen the sides. Remove the metal rings, drizzle with any remaining raspberry coulis and decorate each cheesecake with fresh raspberries and mint leaves.

VARIATION
Ginger and Raspberry Ripple Mini Cheesecakes
Swap half or all of the digestive biscuits for ginger snap biscuits.

EASY BANANA AND STRAWBERRY ICE CREAM

Make instant ice cream from frozen bananas and strawberries: it couldn't be simpler.

250g/9oz banana, sliced
250g/9oz strawberries, washed
  and hulled
1–2 tbsp maple syrup

Put the sliced banana and hulled strawberries in a plastic container and freeze for 4 hours, or until frozen solid.

Tip the frozen fruit into a food processor with the maple syrup and blitz until smooth and creamy.

Serve at once or freeze until needed.

VARIATION
Easy Banana and Berry Ice Cream
Replace the strawberries with frozen mixed berries (e.g. strawberries, raspberries and blueberries).

LITTLE BRIOCHE BREAD AND BUTTER PUDDINGS

Bread and butter pudding never seems to go out of fashion – it's such a classic British dessert. I like to make mini versions with buttery brioche slices and homemade custard for that extra yum factor.

---

4 thick slices of brioche (about 150g/5oz)
25g/1oz softened butter
50g/2oz sultanas
2 tbsp demerara sugar

CUSTARD
1 egg
250ml/8fl oz whole milk
25g/1oz caster sugar

Preheat the oven to 160°C/325°F/Gas 3.

Spread the brioche slices with the softened butter on one side only, then cut each slice into 2 triangles.

Arrange the buttered brioche triangles in 4 large ramekins and sprinkle over the sultanas.

Whisk all the custard ingredients together in a bowl then pour the custard over the brioche in the ramekins and leave for 20 minutes.

Sprinkle each serving with demerara sugar and place the ramekins on a baking sheet.

Bake in the oven for 20 minutes, until the puddings are golden and the custard is set. Remove from the oven and serve straight away.

The baked mini puddings can be frozen (once cooled) for up to 2 months. Defrost, then reheat in the oven at 160°C/325°F/Gas 3 for about 10 minutes, or until heated through.

CHAPTER 7

HOLIDAY COOKING WITH KIDS

BUNNY MARBLE CAKE

Have your family hopping to the table for a slice of this impressive Easter cake. This seasonal showstopper is deceptively simple, so little hands can help create it.

MARBLE CAKE
175g/6oz softened unsalted butter
175g/6oz caster sugar
170g/6oz self-raising flour
3 large eggs
2 tbsp milk
½ tsp baking powder
grated zest of 1 orange
2 tbsp cocoa powder

ICING AND DECORATION
10g/¼oz softened unsalted butter
175g/6oz icing sugar
2 tbsp cocoa powder
1 tbsp milk
30g/1¼oz plain dark chocolate,
  melted and cooled
15 chocolate Easter bunnies and
  chocolate Easter eggs, to
  decorate

Preheat the oven to 160°C/325°F/Gas 3 and line a 23cm/9in deep cake tin with baking parchment.

Put the butter, caster sugar, flour, eggs, milk and baking powder in a mixing bowl and whisk using an electric hand-held whisk until well combined (or use a stand mixer). Divide the mixture equally between 2 bowls.

Add the orange zest to one bowl and the cocoa powder to the other and fold into each cake batter thoroughly.

Put spoons of each of the cake batters into the lined tin in alternate-colour blobs, then create a marble effect by swirling a skewer through the mixtures.

Bake in the oven for 35 minutes until the cake is well risen and coming away from the sides of the tin and a skewer inserted into the middle of the cake comes out clean.

Remove from the oven and leave to cool on a wire rack.

To make the icing, beat the butter, icing sugar, cocoa powder and milk together in a bowl until light and fluffy. Stir in the melted chocolate until well combined.

Put the cooled cake on a cake stand. Spread the icing over the top and down the sides. Arrange the bunnies around the edge of the cake and the chocolate eggs on top. Tie a bow around the bunnies, if necessary, to help hold them in place.

EASTER CUPCAKES

Round up your little chickens and have an egg-cellent time making these adorable cakes, which are fun for the whole family to decorate.

CUPCAKES
125g/4½oz softened unsalted
    butter
2 large eggs
125g/4½oz self-raising flour
125g/4½oz caster sugar
2 tbsp milk
grated zest of 1 lemon
1 tsp baking powder

ICING
100g/3½oz softened unsalted
    butter
175g/6oz icing sugar
1 tbsp lemon juice

TO DECORATE
FOR THE CHICK:
Cheerios
ready-made orange fondant icing
red jelly beans
edible eyes

FOR THE SHEEP:
ready-made black fondant icing
edible eyes
mini marshmallows

Preheat the oven to 160°C/325°F/Gas 3 and line a 12-hole muffin tin with small paper cases.

Put all the cupcake ingredients in a large mixing bowl and whisk with an electric hand-held whisk until light and fluffy (or use a stand mixer). Divide the cake mixture evenly between the paper cases and bake in the oven for 18–20 minutes until well risen and lightly golden brown.

Remove from the oven and leave to cool for a few minutes in the tin before transferring to a wire rack to cool completely.

Beat the icing ingredients together in a bowl with an electric hand-held whisk, then spread the icing over the cooled cupcakes.

To make the chick, put 2 eyes onto an iced cupcake. Make an orange beak and 2 feet out of fondant icing. Push Cheerios into the icing to make the feathers, then add the beak and feet. Put 2 red jelly beans above the eyes. Repeat with 5 more cupcakes.

To make the sheep, create sheep heads and ears with the black fondant icing. Place a face and 2 ears on the icing of one cupcake and stick 2 eyes onto the face with icing. Push mini marshmallows into the icing to make the sheep's wool. Repeat with 5 more cupcakes.

You can freeze the undecorated cupcakes for up to 2 months. Defrost at room temperature.

DRESSED-UP CUPCAKES

These smart cakes are bound to delight dads on Father's Day – just make sure ties are loosened and they are enjoyed in holiday mode!

CUPCAKES
2 large eggs
125g/4½oz softened unsalted
   butter
125g/4½oz caster sugar
1 tbsp milk
100g/3½oz self-raising flour
25g/1oz cocoa powder

ICING
125g/4½oz softened unsalted
   butter
150g/5oz icing sugar
2 tbsp cocoa powder
50g/2oz dark chocolate, broken
   into pieces

white, blue, green and yellow
   fondant icing, to decorate

Preheat the oven to 160°C/325°F/Gas 3 and line a 12-hole muffin tin with 12 paper cases.

Put all the cupcake ingredients in a large bowl and whisk with an electric hand-held whisk until light and fluffy (or use a stand mixer). Divide the cake mixture evenly among the paper cases and bake in the oven for 20–25 minutes until well risen and lightly golden brown. Remove from the oven and leave to cool for a few minutes before transferring to a wire rack to cool completely.

To make the icing, whisk the butter and icing sugar in a bowl with an electric hand-held whisk. Add the cocoa powder and whisk again.

Melt the chocolate in a heatproof bowl over a pan of simmering water (making sure the bottom of the bowl isn't touching the water), then stir it into the icing. Pipe the icing on top of the cakes using a piping bag fitted with a fluted nozzle or spread it with a spatula or spoon.

Roll out some white fondant icing to a thickness of 3mm/⅛in. Slice it into 12 strips and fold to make little shirt collars. Place the collars on top of the icing. Roll out coloured fondant to a thickness of 2mm/⅛in and cut out ties to add to the shirt. Decorate the ties with spots and stripes.

FRUIT FLOWER POTS

When fruit is this fun it will be no trouble getting your family to eat their five-a-day! This makes a healthy treat for Mum on Mother's Day.

1 small watermelon
½ pineapple
150g/5oz blueberries
200g/7oz red seedless grapes

YOU WILL ALSO NEED:
small star or flower cutters
small melon baller
cocktail sticks
6 small plastic cups
6 cake pop sticks

Cut the watermelon in half and cut a 2cm/¾in slice off one of the halves. Stamp out 3 stars or flowers out of the slice. Scoop out balls of watermelon from the other half using a small melon baller.

Remove the skin and core of the pineapple and cut two 2cm/¾in slices off the pineapple. Stamp out 3 stars or flowers using the cutters. Slice the remaining pineapple into cubes.

Break 6 cocktail sticks in half. Insert a cocktail stick into the middle of each flower and push a blueberry onto the stick to make the centre.

Insert a cake pop stick into the flowers to make the stems.

Put a cube of pineapple into the bottom of each cup. Divide the grapes, melon balls, pineapple and blueberries between the cups. Insert the cake pop stick into the pineapple to hold it up in the cup.

THANKSGIVING TURKEY PLATTER

A Thanksgiving five-a-day feast for the whole family to gobble up and there's no cooking required.

3 large slices of pre-sliced edam cheese (from a packet)
1 large slice of pre-sliced Red Leicester cheese
250g/9oz sugar snap peas
1 red pepper, deseeded and cut into strips
125g/4½oz sliced cooked turkey, sliced in half and then folded in half
10 mini pittas, cut into sticks
½ cucumber, sliced
12 cherry tomatoes
edible eyes

Make the turkey's body out of cheese: cut a large oval shape out of one slice of edam cheese. Cut a smaller, round shape out of another slice of edam cheese to make the face. Cut 2 wings out of the edam and 2 smaller wings out of the Red Leicester. Make a small beak out of Red Leicester and place on top of the face.

Arrange the sugar snap peas in a large circle on a large round board or plate, arrange pitta sticks inside the sugar snaps, then pepper slices, folded turkey slices and cucumber rounds, then put the tomatoes in the middle. Put the cheese turkey on top of the tomatoes.

HALLOWE'EN GINGERBREAD MUMMIES AND SKELETONS

Little ghosts and ghouls can help their mummies make these frightfully tasty treats!

140g/4¾oz chilled unsalted
   butter, diced
100g/3½oz soft dark brown sugar
300g/11oz plain flour, plus extra
   for dusting
2 tsp ground cinnamon
2 tsp ground ginger
1 tsp bicarbonate of soda
½ tsp mixed spice
½ tsp ground allspice
1 egg, beaten
50g/2oz black treacle
50g/2oz golden syrup
½ tsp fine salt

GINGERBREAD MUMMIES
icing sugar, for dusting
300g/11oz ready-made white
   fondant icing
white icing pen
edible eyes

GINGERBREAD SKELETONS
200g/7oz icing sugar

Preheat the oven to 180°C/350°F/Gas 4 and line 2 baking sheets with baking parchment.

Put the butter, sugar, flour, spices and bicarbonate of soda in a food processor and blitz until the mixture resembles fine breadcrumbs. Whisk the egg, black treacle, syrup and salt in a bowl. Add the wet mixture to the dry ingredients in the food processor and blitz briefly until combined. Transfer the mixture to a clean work surface and knead to form a soft dough. Wrap the dough in clingfilm and chill for 30 minutes.

Roll the chilled dough out on a floured work surface to the thickness of a £1 coin then stamp out 25–30 gingerbread men, re-rolling the dough as necessary.

Place the gingerbread men on the lined baking sheets then chill for 10 minutes.

Bake the chilled gingerbread men in the oven for 15 minutes until lightly browned and firm. Remove from the oven and transfer to a wire rack to cool.

For the gingerbread mummies, dust a work surface with a little icing sugar and roll out the icing until thin. Slice 5mm/¼in strips of icing to make bandages to make the gingerbread men look like mummies. Attach edible eyes to the cookies using an icing pen

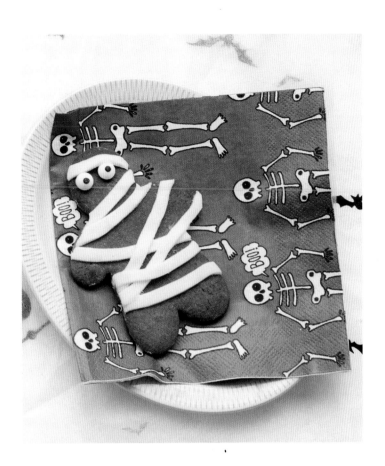

then arrange the lengths of white icing strips as bandages on half of the gingerbread men, trimming the icing as necessary.

For the gingerbread skeletons, mix the icing sugar with a little water until it has a smooth, thick consistency. Spoon the icing into a piping bag fitted with a small round nozzle. Pipe white lines onto the remaining undecorated gingerbread men to make the bones of the skeleton, holding the piping bag at a 45-degree angle just above the gingerbread and squeezing the icing with a constant pressure. Don't move the piping bag until the icing has met the surface. Leave to set for 30 minutes.

The undecorated cookies can be frozen for up to 2 months. Defrost at room temperature.

MINI MONSTER FRIDGE CAKES

Let your mini monsters loose in the kitchen to make this fabulous fridge cake. It's fang-tastic enough to please the whole family.

75g/3oz unsalted butter
100g/3½oz golden syrup
200g/7oz dark chocolate,
  broken into pieces
30g/1¼oz caster sugar
100g/3½oz dried apricots,
  finely chopped
150g/5oz digestive biscuits,
  crushed in a plastic bag with
  a rolling pin
25g/1oz Rice Krispies
100g/3½oz milk chocolate,
  broken into pieces

DECORATION
mini Smarties
edible eyes
writing icing pens

Line a 23cm/9in square baking tin with baking parchment.

Put the butter, golden syrup, dark chocolate and sugar in a saucepan over a low heat and stir until melted, then add the apricots, crushed biscuits and Rice Krispies. Stir to coat the biscuits and Krispies in the sticky mixture, then spoon into the tin and level the top. Cover and chill in the fridge for 1–2 hours until firm.

Once firm, melt the milk chocolate in a heatproof bowl over a pan of simmering water (making sure the bottom of the bowl isn't touching the water). Spread the milk chocolate over the chilled cake mixture and smooth the top. Put back into the fridge for 30 minutes until set firm, then remove from the tin and slice into 12 small rectangular pieces.

Stick edible eyes on each rectangle with icing pens, decorate the body with mini Smarties and draw on an icing mouth.

RUDOLPH POTATOES

Put some seasonal sparkle into your spuds and add a festive twist to this family favourite.

2 baking potatoes
2 small sweet potatoes
olive oil, for brushing (optional)
4 spring onions, chopped
30g/1oz cheddar cheese, grated
2 slices of cooked turkey, finely diced
2 cherry tomatoes
4 edible eyes
pretzels for antlers

Prick the potatoes several times with a fork and cook them in the microwave for 10–12 minutes until soft. Alternatively, brush them with oil and cook them on a baking tray in an oven preheated to 170°C/335°F/Gas 3: the sweet potatoes will need about 45 minutes and the potatoes about 1 hour (or until they feel soft when pressed).

Leave the potatoes to cool for 4–5 minutes, then halve the sweet potatoes and scoop the cooked potato out into a bowl. Cut a round out of the top of the white potatoes and scoop out the inside, leaving a 1.5cm/¾in border. Mix both potatoes together with the spring onions, cheese and turkey. Spoon back into the white potato shells.

Attach the tomatoes to the potatoes to make noses using cocktail sticks and add the edible eyes and broken pretzel pieces for the antlers. Serve straight away (taking care to remove the cocktail sticks).

DOUGHBALL CHRISTMAS WREATH

Pizza pizzazz for the party season, this spectacular Christmas wreath is made with delicious dough balls stuffed with cheese and decorated with tomato sauce, mozzarella and basil.

75g/3oz cheddar cheese, cut into 12 cubes
100g/3½oz mozzarella, cut into 6 slices
bunch of fresh basil, to serve

DOUGH BALLS
350g/12oz strong white flour, plus extra for dusting
7g/¼oz fast-action dried yeast
2 tbsp olive oil, plus extra for greasing
1 tsp fine salt
1 egg, beaten

TOMATO AND BASIL SAUCE
1 tbsp olive oil
1 onion, finely chopped
1 garlic clove, crushed
400g/14oz tin chopped tomatoes
1 tbsp tomato puree
pinch of sugar
1 tbsp chopped fresh basil leaves

To make the dough, put the flour, yeast, oil and salt in a large bowl with 250ml/8fl oz tepid water. Mix together to form a dough then knead on a floured work surface for 5 minutes until smooth and no longer sticky. Place in an oiled bowl, cover with clingfilm and leave to rise in a warm place for 1–2 hours until doubled in size.

While the dough is rising, make the sauce. Heat the oil in a saucepan over a medium heat, add the onion and fry for 5 minutes until softened. Add the garlic and fry for 30 seconds, then add the tomatoes, tomato puree and sugar. Simmer for 10 minutes until reduced and thickened. Remove from the heat and leave to cool.

Preheat the oven to 200°C/400°F/Gas 6 and line a baking sheet with baking parchment.

Knock back the dough on a work surface, then divide it into 12 equal-sized pieces. Roll each piece into a ball and push a cube of cheese inside each ball, making sure it's enclosed fully in the dough so it won't leak out when it melts.

Place the cheese-stuffed dough balls on the lined baking sheet, making a circle of dough balls with a small gap between each ball. Brush them with beaten egg and bake in the oven for 20–25 minutes. Remove from the oven.

Top alternate dough balls with a spoonful of tomato sauce or a slice of mozzarella and put back in the oven for 5 minutes to melt the cheese.

Once cooked, carefully loosen the base of the dough balls using a spatula, slide off the baking sheet onto a serving plate and decorate with fresh basil leaves.

INDEX

CONVERSION CHARTS

WEIGHT

Imperial	Metric	Imperial	Metric
¼oz	10g	13oz	375g
½oz	15g	14oz	400g
¾oz	20g	15oz	425g
1oz	25g	16oz (1lb)	450g
1½oz	40g	1lb 2oz	500g (0.5kg)
2oz	50g	1¼lb	550g
2¼oz	60g	1lb 5oz	600g
2¾oz	70g	1½lb	675g
3oz	75g	1lb 10oz	725g
3½oz	100g	1¾lb	800g
4oz	115g	1lb 14oz	850g
4½oz	125g	2lb	900g
4¾oz	140g	2¼lb	1kg
5oz	150g	2½lb	1.1kg
5½oz	160g	2¾lb	1.25kg
6oz	175g	3lb	1.3kg
7oz	200g	3¼lb	1.5kg
8oz	225g	3½lb	1.6kg
9oz	250g	4lb	1.8kg
9½oz	275g	4½lb	2kg
11oz	300g	5lb	2.25kg
12oz	350g	5½lb	2.5kg

SPOONS (LIQUIDS)

1 tsp	5ml
1 dsp	10ml
1 tbsp (3 tsp)	15ml

NB: 1 Australian tbsp = 20ml (4 tsp)

CONVERSION CHARTS

VOLUME

Imperial	Metric	Imperial	Metric	Imperial	Metric
¼ tsp	1.25ml	7fl oz	200ml	20fl oz (1 UK pint)	600ml
½ tsp	2.5ml	8fl oz	250ml	1¼ pints (25 fl oz)	700ml
1 tsp	5ml	9fl oz	275ml	1½ pints (30 fl oz)	850ml
1 dsp	10ml	10fl oz	300ml	1¾ pints (35 fl oz)	1 litre
1 tbsp	15ml	(½ Imperial pint)		2 pints (40 fl oz)	1.2 litres
1fl oz (2 tbsp)	30ml	11fl oz	325ml	2¼ pints	1.3 litres
2fl oz	50ml	12fl oz	350ml	2½ pints	1.4 litres
3fl oz	75ml	13fl oz	375ml	3 pints	1.75 litres
3½fl oz	100ml	14fl oz	400ml	3½ pints	2 litres
4fl oz	125ml	15fl oz (¾ pint)	450ml	5 pints	3 litres
5fl oz (¼ UK pint)	150ml	16fl oz (1 US pint)	475ml	6 pints	3.6 litres
6fl oz	175ml	18fl oz	500ml		

LENGTH

1 in = 2.5cm; 1 ft = 30.4cm

Imperial	Metric	Imperial	Metric
⅛in	3mm	4in	10cm
¼in	5mm	4½in	12cm
½in	1cm	5in	13cm
¾in	2cm	6in	15cm
1in	2.5cm or 2–3cm	6½in	17cm
1¼in	3cm	7in	18cm
1½in	4cm	8in	20cm
2in	5cm	9in	23cm
2½in	6cm	9½in	24cm
2¾in	7cm	10in	25cm
3in	8cm	12in (1 ft)	30cm
3½in	9cm		

Over the last 25 plus years I've transformed the way parents feed their children, supporting millions of families around the world with my recipes, advice and ranges of chilled and frozen toddler ready meals and organic baby purees. For even more inspiration, visit www.annabelkarmel.com or download my bestselling Baby & Toddler Recipes app.

Annabel Karmel, MBE

With expertise spanning more than 25 years, London-born mother of three Annabel Karmel reigns as the UK's No.1 children's cookery author, best-selling international author, and a world-leading expert on devising delicious, nutritious meals for babies, children and families.

Since launching her first book in 1991, a cookbook born out of her own son's fussy eating habits, Annabel has been credited with starting a food revolution with her tasty recipes and simple methods. She has since gone on to write 43 more cookbooks, which have sold more than 6 million copies worldwide and people of all ages now rely on Britain's original 'mumpreneur' for the best mealtimes.

In 2006, Annabel received an MBE in the Queen's Birthday Honours for her outstanding work in the field of child nutrition, and she is also well recognised as one of the UK's leading female entrepreneurs.

With millions of families relying on Annabel's recipes to raise healthy, happy babies, the feeding expert has cooked-up a brand new edition of her bestselling Baby & Toddler Recipes app. Packed with more than 220 delicious, nutritious recipes, simple planners, shopping lists, and more, it's the handiest of guides for easy mealtime inspiration – whether you're cooking for baby, toddler or the whole family.

You'll also discover Annabel in the supermarket aisles with her nutritious Organic Baby Purees, Chilled Toddler Meals and Frozen Kids Meals. Inspired by her most popular cookbook recipes, they taste just like you'd make at home – perfect for those busy days.

For lots more exclusive recipes, tips and advice, plus a host of great competitions and offers, join the AK Club for free today at www.annabelkarmel.com. You can also be a part of Annabel's world on social media:

annabelkarmeluk

annabelkarmel

annabelkarmel

ACKNOWLEDGEMENTS

THANKS TO:

Lucinda McCord, Jonathan Lloyd of Curtis Brown, Stephen Margolis, Nicholas, Lara and Scarlett Karmel, Evelyn Etkind, Marina Abaigon Magpoc, Mel Diamond, Lucy Staley, Carole Tonkinson, Martha Burley, Katy Denny, Laura Nickoll, Nikki Dupin and Abby Cocovini from Studio Nic&Lou, Clare Winfield, Eliora McDonald, Elizabeth Denny and Florence Dupin.

And thanks to our cover-star finalists: Teddy Tang, Edith Scott, Harry and Ava Wing-King, Aura Willow Walsh and Parker Brannigan-Warren.